# BUILDING A CHURCH
# OF SMALL GROUPS

**Also by Bill Donahue and Russ Robinson**
*Leading Life-Changing Small Groups*
*The Seven Deadly Sins of Small Group Ministry*

BILL**DONAHUE** RUSS**ROBINSON**

# BUILDING A CHURCH
# OF SMALL GROUPS

a place

where

nobody

stands

alone

**ZONDERVAN**™

GRAND RAPIDS, MICHIGAN 49530 USA

WILLOW
Willow Creek Resources

# ZONDERVAN™

*Building a Church of Small Groups*
Copyright © 2001 by Willow Creek Association

Requests for information should be addressed to:

Zondervan, *Grand Rapids, Michigan 49530*

**Library of Congress Cataloging-in-Publication Data**

Donahue, Bill.
   Building a church of small groups : a place where nobody stands alone / Bill Donahue and Russ Robinson.
      p. cm.
   Includes bibliographical references.
   ISBN-13: 978-0-310-26710-2
   ISBN-10: 0-310-26710-2
  1. Church group work.  2. Small groups—Religious aspects—Christianity.
  I. Robinson, Russ  II. Title.
   BV652.2 D65 2001
   253'.7—dc21

2001026969

*Interior design by Beth Shagene*

*Printed in the United States of America*

07 08 09 10 11 12 /❖ DCI/ 10 9 8 7 6 5 4

# Contents

# Foreword

George Bernard Shaw once famously remarked, "Those who can, do. Those who cannot, teach."

The same, I suppose, often holds true for writing. But not in this case.

Community has become one of those topics which, like the weather, everybody discusses but not many folks do anything about. But Bill Donahue and Russ Robinson have not just thought and read and talked about community. They have rolled up their sleeves and devoted their vocational lives to figuring out how to actually help make it happen with real-life people in a real-life church.

Robert Wuthnow, a social scientist at Princeton, has written that the small groups movement is the biggest social revolution of our day. But he says that the small groups movement is not just creating community; it is changing its fundamental nature, all too often in less than optimal ways. People often approach small groups involvement with a mindset that says, "Come if you can. Leave when you must. Should things get inconvenient or messy, you can always bail out."

Community in a church is to be a far different experience. It's not like whitewall tires; it's not an optional item. The challenge is to make Christian community a covenental experience in a consumeristic world.

This is where Russ and Bill's role as practitioners and not just theoreticians is critical. They don't just know the textbooks; they've been in the lab. Building community in churches requires a firm grasp on a theology of the church. But it also requires a kind of knowledge about working with people that comes only through experience. How do you spot effective leaders? How do you nurture and train them to serve in the midst of busy lives? How do you make small group life sustainable for a congregation of people who are worshiping, evangelizing, raising children, and holding down jobs—doing all the stuff of life? How do you keep difficult people from blowing up a group? (This is where Russ and Bill have special expertise, because one of them is in fact a difficult person.)

It has been my privilege to serve alongside Bill and Russ for many years as we seek to build community at our church. It's my privilege now to introduce you to their work so that together we can all labor more effectively.

—JOHN ORTBERG

# Acknowledgments

This book is ultimately a story. Its setting is this remarkable laboratory—Willow Creek Community Church—in which we have experimented and learned about small groups for the past decade. The cast of characters, too numerous to mention, all played a role in the drama of Willow Creek becoming a church of small groups. So our acknowledgements begin with many apologies to all those we won't credit by name. As you in our church family read this, you can be assured that almost every sentence brings a face to mind, and our feelings were ones of frequent thanks for and awe at what God has done through you.

We know how little of our dream of community would have happened without the vision and values for it in the leadership and teaching of Dr. B (Gil Belizekian), Bill Hybels, and John Ortberg, and the support and investment of Willow Creek's Elders and Board of Directors. They have made our church one where we could lead together toward a common vision of an ever more inclusive community.

The vision could never approach reality without an army of Area Leaders and Ministry Directors, Division Leaders, staff and volunteer Coaches, and servant-driven Small Group Leaders engaging in the daily battle to give everyone who calls Willow their church home a place in community. And had we not been given the head start of years of being a church with terrific small groups, thanks to Don Cousins, Mark Weinert, and their staff and volunteer teams, it is doubtful we would have made it to what we'll share in this book.

The fingerprints of pioneers like Jim Dethmer, Jon Wallace, Greg Hawkins, Brett Eastman and John Burke are all over what we write too. Marge Anderson, Rob Stevens, Deb Beise, Judson Poling, and many others in our Ministry Services Department, most often behind the scenes, advanced their efforts. We stand on tall shoulders in writing this story.

We also owe much to several readers, inside and outside Willow Creek—those "unfortunate" enough to be in our small groups or our circle of friends as we wrote—whose reading of early manuscripts helped make this book more useful and clear. You will be seeing many stories of churches too; their leaders made sure we were telling their stories and ours in realistic but relevant ways. Our interns, Joe Besenjak and Sandra Unger, kept us on line with some of our theology and described practice.

Two publishing teams joined forces to make this project happen. The Willow Creek Association provided Joe Sherman, Doug Yonamine, Christine Anderson, and others whenever we needed them to steer us in the right direction on everything from content to logistics. Zondervan blessed us with Jack Kuhatchek, our small groups fellow-zealot, and his "best in class" staff to wring as much potential out of this project as possible. Keri Kent deserves thanks for helping us gather stories. Joan Huyser-Honig was our angel of mercy; she gave this book as much of one voice as is possible with two authors and edited the original manuscript with excellence and passion for the subject matter.

We always owe a debt of gratitude to our assistants, Joan Oboyski and Karen Bell. Not only did they chase down what we needed along the way for the book; they also kept the rest of our ministry work flowing at points where the project required attention, so we could remain practitioners with you who read what we are learning. And they did it with excellence and self-sacrifice we can never praise adequately.

Finally, there are seven people who paid privately but generously to make this project happen. Our wives and kids—Gail, Ryan, and Kinsley; and Lynn, Phil, Mark, and Tim—made do without us at times yet cheered us on when it got hard. Gail and Lynn gave of their time and ideas as they read the freshest drafts, and lived well with the interruptions and emergencies the past year produced. Without their belief, support, and love, we would never have been able to tell of the place we are trying to create together: a church where nobody stands alone.

—BILL DONAHUE AND RUSS ROBINSON

# Introduction
## The Willow Creek Story

Founded in 1975 in a suburban Chicago movie theater, Willow Creek Community Church has become one of the most visible, multifaceted ministries in the United States. The church quickly became known for its creative weekend "seeker services," designed to present timeless Christian truths via culturally relevant means: drama, music, video, dance, and biblical messages. Almost nonstop growth multiplied the varied ways we met the needs of seekers and believers—through ministries to children and adults, singles and couples, mature Christians, new converts, and families in crisis. Our congregation of over 20,000 now touches thousands of churches in its role as a "teaching church" through the worldwide Willow Creek Association ministry.

But in 1991, Willow Creek faced a crisis that touched every ministry in the church. It sounds simple enough now: the people that we had worked so hard to win to Christ were having an increasingly difficult time making the church a part of their life and making themselves a part of the church's life. In many cases people couldn't connect meaningfully to the church. We had small groups as a ministry within the church, but only about ten to fifteen percent of our total congregation could get connected into one of those smaller settings. We were a large, growing church with a genuine problem of connecting people to the church and caring for them.

Willow Creek made a bold declaration in 1992: that we would become a church where no one stands alone. But to accomplish that goal, we knew that we needed to have a place where true community could exist. *Community* is a popular word and can mean a lot of things. For the Christian, it essentially means being Christ to one another, sharing the fullness of his life with everyone we meet. Dietrich Bonhoeffer said it this way, "It means, first, that a Christian needs others because of Jesus Christ.

It means, second, that a Christian comes to others only through Jesus Christ. It means, third, that in Jesus Christ we have been chosen from eternity, accepted in time, and united for eternity."[1]

We were not experiencing that kind of community throughout the entire church. And Bill Hybels, our senior pastor, knew this. Bill had always dreamed of building a biblically functioning community. Instead, we had become what he described as "a federation of sub-ministries." In effect, we were a bunch of parachurch ministries with the same address. Each of us was gathering people to his or her own ministry area and beginning to build lots of programs and events around the gathering. Small groups were ancillary. We knew we had to make a change.

A team of us gathered to dream a dream: What would the local church look like if it really got serious about biblical community and made it accessible to everyone? With this vision and the challenge to extend Christ's life and ministry to each person within our church's reach, we followed our God-inspired dream. We began moving from a church where small groups were optional to a church where small groups defined the core organizational strategy. Willow Creek made sure everyone in the entire church had the opportunity for transforming relationships—by becoming a church of small groups.

In making that decision, we underestimated the size of our task. On the surface everything in the church seemed fine at the time. Our weekend service attendance averaged 12,000. About 1,800 adults were in 200 "disciple-making" groups. Our weekend seeker services, designed to present a creative, compelling gospel to unchurched people, were attracting many lost people, and we baptized hundreds each year. Mid-week believers' services (the "New Community") gathered about 4,500 adults for worship, prayer, Bible teaching, and the sacraments. Members were using their gifts in service, dozens of ministries were up and running, and the church had just completed an expansion that would soon be totally paid for, leaving us with $50 million in debt-free facilities on 135 acres of land. Church leaders from around the world were beginning to come to conferences organized by the newly-formed Willow Creek Association (WCA). It seemed like things could not be better.

But beneath this vital ministry, stress fractures were forming in our church's relational foundation. Bill Hybels recalls, "We were building a twenty-story building on a ten-story foundation, and soon it began to give way." I (Russ) remember sitting in elder board meetings—I served four years as one of Willow Creek's ten elders—pondering this conundrum. Our blessings of growth had become a kind of curse, which embroiled us in a love/hate set of decisions. We loved the movement of the Holy Spirit, the changed lives, the catalytic energy, the sense of awe as we saw God at work; but we hated the disorderly organizational dynamics, burned-out staff and lay leadership, displaced people, and undiscipled masses.

Evangelistic growth, new ministries with thousands of volunteers, and the increasing need to disciple existing members and new Christ followers presented us with an overwhelming challenge. We were at risk of losing the "Community" in Willow Creek Community Church. Though we had not lost the value of community or the expression of it in some areas of the church, we had to find a better way to intentionalize the practice of community to ensure that life-giving transformation was taking place.

We knew community was not optional, and we knew many people craved it. But we had no accessible means for many of them to participate in it. We studied Carl George's strategy for what he calls the "meta-church" and decided to take the plunge by piloting the model in a few ministry areas. After seeing life after life change and after working through some of the initial (and substantial) barriers to change, we made an irrevocable commitment to redesign Willow Creek with community life at the core. Small groups—once a department—would now become a way of doing life and ministry.

Since we made that commitment, we have thrown everything we had at this effort: intense and frequent prayer, money, energy, perseverance, and countless hours of personal meetings with people, sharing our dream and urging their commitment. We gently invited and boldly exhorted, we envisioned and implored, we modeled and trained, laughed and cried, and sometimes wondered if it was worth it.

But we did not wonder long. Each story of life-change, every new conversion, every marriage rebuilt, each broken life mended, and every new spiritual gift discovered and deployed for kingdom advancement shouted to us: "It is worth it!" Moreover, the life and ministry of Christ, who created us for community, reminded us that the cause was well worth the cost. After all, he had paid a dear price to establish the first redemptive community—the church. To pursue anything less would grieve the One whose boundless love snatched us from eternal isolation from all that is good.

The end result is that since 1992, Willow Creek has gone from a church *with* small groups—that is, small groups being one of our programs—to being a church *of* small groups. Instead of ten to fifteen percent of the congregation connected into a small group, we have become a place where over 18,000 individuals are connected in 2,700 small groups.

In every church ministry, including elders, board of directors, and management team, we strive for authentic community through group life. We put everyone in small groups: children or adult, divorced or married, intellectual or athlete, buster or boomer, new convert or veteran Christ follower. Whoever you are at Willow Creek, we can connect you into a small group. We have become a church body with a small groups skeleton.

This book describes that adventure. Our goal is to share the lessons learned (several), the mistakes made (innumerable), and the steps necessary to build a biblically functioning community of Christ followers who live out the practice of community and relational integrity. We will offer guidelines, decisions, warnings, and wisdom for you to apply in the context of your church setting.

■

This book is designed so that key leaders in your church can understand why you are leading them—if you so choose—toward becoming a church of small groups. It contains practical and proven principles from our experience at Willow Creek and those of other churches. Pastors, elders, deacons, bishops, small group leaders, teachers, and others committed to growing the local church will benefit. We hope you will share it with your team and discuss it with the leaders around you. Much is at stake, and it is important for church leaders at all levels to grasp the significance of what this can mean for their church.

Part 1 presents theological and human evidence to build the case for small groups. As in your church, people asked us, "Why do we need groups? Aren't we doing OK? After all, we are growing and making disciples; why do we need another program?" The truth is, you do not need another program—and neither did we. What we did need as a body was the fully unadulterated expression of the communal life experienced in the Trinity, designed in Creation, practiced by Christ, and intended for the local church. We will help you and your church get their arms around the call to community.

In Part 2, we move from vision to practice. It may surprise you to find us moving all the way from the macro picture of biblical community to the micro perspective of an individual small group. Our experience is that, unless we take the vision of oneness into the practical realm of small group life, we haven't faced what our churches must pursue. This section defines the term *small group*. It describes how the big idea of community finds its deepest expression in the little community, where the average small group member begins to see what God knows and dreams for them.

Part 3 tells how to deploy leaders. We'll explain how to identify and recruit small group leaders, train them for effective service, and then coach and support them so their service is long term.

Part 4 helps you envision the changes your church must make if you want to build a church *of* small groups. It pinpoints five key decisions you'll face during the transition. You'll learn six core principles necessary to any change strategy, no matter which model you choose for building small groups. Finally, this section discusses how to phase in small groups.

One last word: tackling this challenge will be the hardest thing you've ever done. The church is complex enough without introducing a whole new way of building its infrastructure. Since any small group ministry is about people, you will face inevitable challenges. You cannot achieve your goal without change, so get ready for a long-haul effort.

Not just the story of Willow Creek, this is the story of countless other churches—and yours as well. Included in this book you will find churches—many just like yours—that are pursuing biblical community through small groups. Among them you will find:

- a 128-year-old traditional Lutheran church that has changed dramatically over the last five years to embrace community at the deepest levels
- a young new church in the inner city of Chicago that is reaching a new generation
- a church in Texas that has discovered how to revolutionize the community, one neighborhood at a time
- a Presbyterian church that understands how commitment to the local church means commitment to a small community of Christ followers
- a church in Pennsylvania that has come to understand that leadership development and coaching those leaders is the whole ball game

Church after church, story after story. We have only captured a few of them, but we think you will find some of your story woven into theirs, and in this you will find hope and inspiration. As these churches found, the goal requires hard work—but the benefit is well worth the cost. You will experience, personally and in your church, what it means to live in community as God intends. You will be amazed at how small groups can transform people. Whatever your church was doing well will be leveraged for even greater gains. Both the joy of the journey and the exhilaration of the destination make it all worthwhile! Especially when you know God's vision for oneness. . . .

# MAKING THE CASE
# FOR COMMUNITY

Part 1

Lawyers live for closing arguments. There is no exception: those who enjoy trying cases love launching into their closing argument. It's something I (Russ) looked forward to whenever I tried a case during my legal career, which lasted from 1982 through the mid-1990s.

I still remember the thrill of making my closing statement in a personal injury case I tried almost fifteen years ago. We had been on trial for almost a week, had submitted all our witness testimony and evidence, and were ready to address the jury. I tweaked my previously prepared remarks during a break. My opponent went first, speaking on behalf of the plaintiff, a large corporation, that had sued my clients—a young couple whose alleged negligence had caused their company damage.

Then it was my turn. The other side had made good arguments, but I knew the jury members' sympathies, the law, and the facts were all on my side. During that closing argument, all my work—during law school, earlier trials, and preparation for this case—came together. My client, and even the opposing lawyer, later commented that I had the jury eating out of my hand. There are few thrills like delivering a closing argument.

Lawsuits sometimes last years, but all the investigation, witness interviews, and evidence development culminates in those few minutes of making a final plea before deliberations begin. The jury or judge has listened and weighed nuances while attorneys present evidence and witnesses for both sides. The judge has made her rulings; the parties have rested their cases; the stage is set. At that moment, every trial attorney knows the pressure is on; there's one last chance before the verdict is rendered. The outcome may well rise and fall on this moment of closing argument.

We have framed the first part of this book as a closing argument. Your decision about community, about building a church of small groups, and about your own leadership may rest on your decisions about what you read in the next three chapters. We will make the case that, unless you begin with a crystal clear vision for community, you will not succeed in moving your church or yourself toward small groups.

We pull together a wide variety of evidence, mostly from the Bible, into a closing argument that makes the case for community. As we begin our journey to building a church of small groups, we aim to persuade you that this vision is far more than a clever design for assimilation. We build our case for small groups from the mind and the heart of God himself, for God's own words about community provide the best possible evidence.

Our motivation is simple. Both as laypeople and church staff members, we have found we can rely for a time on purely human drive to keep doing ministry. But experience, a hard taskmaster, has taught us that human ideas—program concepts, good management strategies, and the like—cannot sustain in us the energy we need to become a church of small groups.

The more we've come to understand, however, that community is essential in God's identity, mind, and dream for us, the more we draw fresh energy for ministry. We hope that, by the time we finish our closing argument, you will discover a fresh understanding of community and endless energy for accomplishing it through ministry.

Our case for becoming a church of small groups begins with theological evidence, the study of God (chapter 1). Next we focus on the sociological evidence, who we are as God's creatures and why we need small groups (chapter 2). Finally, we present organizational evidence for why small groups are the best way a church can achieve community (chapter 3).

As the judge would now say, "Mr. Robinson and Mr. Donahue, you may now address the jury. . ."

# In the Beginning, God: The Theological Evidence

*Whatever community exists as a result of God's creation, it is only a reflection of an eternal reality that is intrinsic to the being of God. Because God is eternally one, when he created in his image, he created oneness.*

GILBERT BILEZIKIAN, COMMUNITY 101

"Ladies and gentlemen of the jury. Yours is an awesome responsibility. Soon we will conclude our closing arguments, and you will render the verdict. Our society trusts fallible men and women with decisions like the ones you now face. Soberly and objectively, you must review the evidence. Our arguments are not evidence; you must judge our closing statement to determine how you view the evidence. The verdict will rest with you. But we believe there is clear and convincing proof for building a church of small groups. We'll begin by reviewing the theological evidence for community."

The arguments from theology—that is, the study of God and his person—prove beyond doubt that God's nature is communal. Our theological analysis will show you why God's communal nature requires you to respond by building community—for yourself and for your church.

The theological case depends on three basic ideas. First, God exists in community; he has forever existed as and will into eternity remain three persons in One. Second, God was incarnate in Christ Jesus, whose transformational relationships offer a model you cannot ignore. Third, Jesus dreams of oneness for all Christians, which is why you must move your church toward his vision.

## The God of Community

You've read Genesis 1:26: "Then God said, 'Let us make man in our image, in our likeness. . . .'" But have you noticed its remarkable expressions of plurality? These thirteen words include three references to God's unique nature. Note the references to "us" and "our," which proclaim the core doctrine of the Trinity. At the same time, God's singularity is a core doctrine of the church universal. As Deuteronomy 6:4 says, "Hear, O Israel: The LORD our God, the LORD is one." In other words, God begins Scripture and the creation story with the theological idea of plurality within oneness.

The creation account provides us an amazing window into the nature of the community of God, in whose image we are created. This plurality of beings comes to consensus to create humans in their image. They create in their collective image, which, in part, is a community-bearing image. It is not enough to say God is interested in community or even obsessed with community. God, rightly defined and understood, *is* community.

The doctrine of the Trinity is complex. Orthodox Christians have for generations accepted that God is Three in One, but few of us think much about it. This seemingly enigmatic doctrine of the Trinity, however, has massive implications. As Gareth Icenogle explains:

> The small group is a generic form of human community that is trans-cultural, trans-generational and even transcendant. The call to human gathering in groups is a God-created (ontological) and God-directed (theological) ministry, birthed out of the very nature and purpose of God's being. God as Being exists in community. The natural and simple demonstration of God's communal image for humanity is the gathering of the small group.[1]

Did you catch that? "God's communal image for humanity is the gathering of the small group." The entire Bible proclaims that God (expressed singularly) exists from all time and for all time in community as the Trinity (plurality). This Trinitarian doctrine begins with the creation account, where all three persons of the Trinity are present. When God created the world, "the Spirit of God was hovering over the waters" (Genesis 1:2). John describes Jesus as the agent of Creation: "In the beginning was the Word, and the Word was with God. . . . Through him all things were made; without him nothing was made that has been made" (John

1:1–3). Since God himself lives and works in community and since we are created in God's image, then we too are created in and for community.

You cannot come to understand the true nature of God unless and until you accept that he is not simply an individual. God is, in every sense of the word, a "group" as well. In the biblical framework (see, for example, Matthew 18:15–20), whenever "two or three come together" in God's name, they together have an ability to act in concert for the good of themselves and others. Something unique happens when individuals work together. So it is with God in the Trinity. Without an ounce of sacrilege, we might call the Godhead the first small group!

I (Bill) never fully understood this until I heard Dr. Gilbert Bilezikian first preach on community. He was one of the first theologians to present not only the powerful triune nature of God but also the relational aspects. If you want a vision for the kind of community that Gilbert shared with us, then read *Community 101*. Gilbert describes the community as both vertical and horizontal—just like the bars on a cross. They meet in the center, and true community is born when we experience God and all of his fullness and his people in all of their fullness.

In God there is the identity of the One, and yet there are Three in One. There is distinctive individuality. God exists in community. This picture of the oneness of God shatters our independence.

## The Community Gene

Let's dig deeper into the statement "Let *us* make man in *our* image." What are the implications of being image bearers, ones who bear a likeness to this community defining God?

It is clear what this does not mean. We are not triune deities. (Only a schizoid person says, "I am God, and so am I"!) So we know our image bearing must mean something other than a direct, one-to-one correlation of God's community likeness.

Some might suggest that while God is indeed three persons in One, bearing his image refers to having eternal souls, as distinct from the rest of the creation. That seems an unlikely understanding. If the intent of the passage was to distinguish humans from the rest of creation, the statement among the persons of the Trinity might be more like this: "Let us make man unlike any other creation so far. Let us give him a distinctive spiritual dimension and existence, so humans are unique among the created." But that is not what God says.

In constructing humans, God trumped all his design work. He performed a kind of crowning creative act we don't often grasp. Sure, he gave humans a soul dimension, a spiritual existence that distinguishes us from plants, animals, and other created elements. Then he did more—much, much more. God chose to embed in us a distinct kind of relational DNA. God created us all with a "community gene," an inborn, intentional, inescapable part of what it means to be human.

This "relational DNA" or "community gene" helps explain why churches need small groups. People don't come to church simply to satisfy spiritual needs. They come to us internally wired with a desire for connection. They see church as a likely place to discover God's involvement in creation and in their lives. Their hunger for togetherness is an inescapable mark of humanity. If we treat this hunger casually, we subtly deny the truth of creation. However, when our churches own the responsibility to move people into relationship, we validate the nature of the God whose image we bear. We are created in God's image; therefore, we are created for community. It's part of being an image bearer of God himself.

## Community Transcends Culture

You don't have to be a Christian or churchgoer to understand that people need each other. Prisoners know the pain of being behind bars, away from the community of normal life. They view "solitary confinement" as even worse. Being subjected to extended aloneness kills the spirit, introduces insanity, and destroys a person.

Senator and former Vietnam POW John McCain describes the elation he experienced when he was reunited with fellow prisoners after a horribly long and brutal separation:

> I was overwhelmed by the compulsion to talk nonstop, face-to-face with my obliging new cellmate. I ran my mouth ceaselessly for four days. . . . One of the more amusing spectacles in prison is the sight of two men, both just released from solitary, talking their heads off simultaneously, neither one listening to the other, both absolutely enraptured by the sound of their voices.[2]

We all know the differences between introverts and extroverts. Some of us seek more solitude than others do. Yet, we also know that even introverts need the companionship of other people, because, more than any other creatures, humans are ravenously relational. We seek each other out. We meet, court, and marry. We define life by the community of family. We prize functional families and friends, relationships that are loyal and true, safe and loving. Only the sociopath (defined as one departed from the norm) ultimately rejects relationship. The rest of us—regardless of age, gender, race, temperament, or past history—realize that part of being human means having an insatiable hunger for community.

Paul, apostle to the Gentiles, explains why every society recognizes this human passion for connection. "From the time the world was created, people have seen the earth and sky and all that God made. They can clearly see his invisible qualities—his eternal power and divine nature. So they have no excuse whatsoever for not knowing God" (Romans 1:20 NLT). Since part of that "divine nature" is the plurality of God and his own craving for community, God's created testimony makes it plain to unbelievers that people need each other.

Believers understand that everyone hungers for community, first, because of who God is, and further, because we bear God's communal image. Dallas Willard explains how understanding the doctrine of the Trinity should change our lives:

> . . .nearly every professing Christian has some information about the Trinity, the incarnation, the atonement, and other standard doctrines. But to have the "right" answers about the Trinity, for example, and to actually *believe* in the reality of the Trinity, is all the difference in the world.
>
> The advantage of believing in the reality of the Trinity is not that we get an A from God for giving "the right answer." Remember, to believe something is to act as if it is so. . .the advantage of *believing* in the Trinity is that we then live as if the Trinity is real: as if the cosmos environing us actually is, beyond all else, a self-sufficing community of unspeakably magnificent personal beings of boundless love, knowledge, and power. And, thus believing, our lives naturally integrate themselves, through our actions, into the reality of such a universe, just as with two plus two equals four.[3]

Let's now sum up the first evidence in the theological case for community. God is three and yet One. We are created in God's community-bearing image. Both the Bible and the creation teach us that to be human is to hunger for community. Therefore, if we compromise community within the church, we compromise our essence as created persons.

## Jesus in Community

The second piece of evidence in the theological case for community flows from God's actual entrance into human history. In our own lives we meet God incarnate, that is, God becoming flesh, the "God with us," the Immanuel, Jesus Christ.

Through their accounts of Christ's conduct, the Gospels reveal what it means to bear the created image of the triune God. Jesus' entire public ministry models what it means to live in community. His pattern shows us why community—most particularly, community experienced through small group relationships—is a necessity, not an option, for those of us who bear his name.

You can see the drama of Jesus' relational choices in the third chapter of Mark. Early in his ministry, he drew crowds wherever he went. People heard about the power of his words and deeds, and, as Mark describes, they chased him:

> Jesus withdrew with his disciples to the lake, and a large crowd from Galilee followed. When they heard all he was doing, many people came to him from Judea, Jerusalem, Idumea, and the regions across the Jordan and around Tyre and Sidon. Because of the crowd he told his disciples to have a small boat ready for him, to keep the people from crowding him. For he had healed many, so that those with diseases were pushing forward to touch him. (Mark 3:7–10)

Some of us might seize such a moment to leverage the crowd. Interpreting the large audience as a sure sign of God's presence and anointing, we might try to attract more audience share, step up publicity, explore logistics for handling larger crowds, and propose a building project.

Not Jesus. He did not equate plenty of people with true community. In fact, instead of working the crowd, he muffled it and pulled away. "Jesus went up on a mountainside and called to him those he wanted" (Mark 3:13). Jesus invited twelve men to join him in a three-year, life-transforming, ministry-embedding journey.

His connection with the disciples is a perfect example of relational interdependence. Jesus knew the masses had deep needs. Yet, he spent most of his public ministry doing life and ministry together with his little community of twelve disciples. He drew away from the many, then selected a few to reach the many. As Eugene Peterson explains, "Jesus invested 90 percent of his time with twelve Jewish men so that he could reach all Americans."[4]

Jesus followed the divine pattern of gathering a few so that he would transform many lives. Jesus has existed from all time in the community of Three in One, the gathering of few. It was inevitable—because of his nature and identity—that when Jesus became incarnate as a human being, like us bearing the created image of the triune God, he gathered a few into community.

## Lone Rangers Are Alone Rangers

We've examined two pieces of evidence for community. As created beings we were formed for community. As Christ-followers we are transformed for community. Nevertheless, because our culture emphasizes individualism and self-reliance, many Christians miss the testimony of Christ's life. They think they can be Christlike without pursuing community life.

Many of us in the church view community as optional. As Willow Creek's Director of Small Groups, I (Russ) talk with veteran Christians who resist being connected into what they call "the system." Both long-term "Creekers" and churched people who have moved here decline formal connection to the church or a small group. We lovingly call them "renegades."

Some of them are "church-hopping renegades." Applying consumerism philosophy to their church engagement, they treat Willow Creek like one item on a Chicagoland church buffet. Their agenda is to get themselves and their family "fed,"[5] the tastiness of the entrée the sole measure of whether they will grace our establishment again. Life-transforming community is not part of the nutrition plan.

Granted, the church has done them few favors. We paint a picture of Christianity rightly lived as a simple matter of you and your relationship with God. Such minimalist, "fire insurance" versions of faith may escape hell. But they have nothing to do with following Jesus. Following Jesus means following him into community.

Some people go a little further than an "independent contractor" mindset toward God—to a cheapened version of community sometimes labeled "fellowship." We grew up in several different churches and denominations, all of which fed us fellowship dinners in the fellowship hall during fellowship gatherings. Call it "community lite." While our upbringing provided many good gifts, our malnourished communities dramatically undersold the kind of oneness inherent in the Trinity and modeled by Christ's life.

I (Bill) experienced this starvation diet early in my Christian life. Having come to faith in a church that had no groups, I was eager for community and soon found it in a small group of friends. They had begun a home Bible study to nourish believers and reach seekers. We began to invite lost friends. Soon our Bible study grew to thirty-five people, half of whom did not know Christ. Our experience was unbelievable. Lives were changing, believers were encouraged, and the lost were seeing firsthand what true spiritual community can look like. Then the church shut us down. They worried that too many "publicans and sinners" at church might sway our young people. They feared that our new believers would become like the sinners. It never occurred to them that the reverse might happen. Once again, true community was shelved.

Of course, sometimes we stumbled into deeper Christian friendships, rare and wonderful clues of our God-designed bent toward connection. Sometimes our families gave us a taste of this community. We wondered whether parachurch organizations offered what we sought. Painful as it is to admit, somewhere along the way, the dozen or so otherwise decent churches of which we were a part lost the biblical concept of community as God designed it and as Jesus showed us.

Many churches today lack intentional community life. We love Willow Creek Community Church, but it has sometimes fallen far short of the ideal expressed in a most basic theology. During exponential growth, authentic connection at Willow Creek has at times been the exception rather than the rule. We have far to go before the majority experience what the disciples tasted in Christ's company. It is a huge task to connect a whole church full of people, let alone have them experience community like Jesus knows and models it.

But the evidence from Jesus' life compels us to stay the course, to resist resistance. When the church renders its verdict on Jesus in community, it must remodel its foundation according to Christ's example of group life.

## Discipleship Is about Oneness

There is some consolation in knowing that even Jesus, after a three-year investment in twelve disciples, fell short of what he knew was possible for their community. The way he expressed the shortcoming provides the third piece of evidence in the theological case for small groups.

We find this evidence in John's account of the end of Jesus' ministry. In John 17, Jesus offers an awe-inspiring glimpse of God's ideal for his children: that they live in oneness. The Trinitarian and incarnational evidence is strong; John 17, however, may be the defining piece of evidence in the theological case for small groups. Every lawyer dreams of finding a smoking gun, the surefire proof in a case. If ever there was a smoking gun on community, it is John 17.

Notice the chapter's setting. Jesus is having a final, pre-death, extended conversation with his heavenly Father. The eleven remaining disciples are still gathered around Jesus despite the dismissal of Judas and their own infighting for prominence. They hang on Jesus' every word, having been humbled by slavish foot-washing. We are not sure where they are, whether still at the table or in the Garden of Gethsemane, but Jesus prays to his Father while his friends wait.

This poignant passage gives us an insiders' look at Jesus' prayer. Jesus prays as One who, from and for all time, shares essence of being with God, talking to another with whom he has existed in the most intimate of relationships.

Another factor is at play in this conversation. It is sometimes said that when someone faces death, one's conversation reveals his or her deepest passions, hopes, and dreams. That's why we go out of our way to honor dying wishes. In his final hours, Jesus gives us clues to his chief concerns.

Jesus knows that in a few hours he will become God's ultimate sacrificial lamb. Death is a certainty, save a last-minute move by God to change salvation history. While conversing with his heavenly Father, Jesus speaks penetrating words that show the magnificence he accords this thing we call community. He prays for the band of followers he has gathered, particularly for the disciples with whom he spent the most time modeling community. "I will remain in the world no longer, but they are still in the world, and I am coming to you. Holy Father, protect them by the power of your name—the name you gave me—so that they may be one as we are one" (John 17:11).

"So that they may be one as we are one." If you have any theological sense of what Jesus is saying, you recognize that statement's overwhelming punch. Jesus says, "I want human beings—for example, these men into whom I've poured my life—to find the kind of oneness we experience in the Trinity." The Triune community that is the first community. The Godhead that is the model community. Jesus really thinks this is possible!

What do you do with these words? Note how well Jesus' final conversation with his Father applies to small group ministry, to building community within a local church. Jesus chose a particular way to invest three years of his life in public ministry. He has rallied others to himself, poured his life into them, and now trusts them to extend his people-investment strategy and ministry. On his final night, he asks his heavenly Father for something specific—to grant his community the gift of oneness.

Imagine if Jesus had taken prayer requests from his disciples. Earlier they had asked for positions of honor to the exclusion of others—right-hand man status—or assurances of future security for having thrown in their lot with Jesus. "Overthrow Rome!" they might plead. Some would settle for good fishing weather; others would want the promise of future ministry on the same terms as they had known it. Community? Not in a million years!

But that is what Jesus asks of God. He asks for them to know oneness. Not just any kind of oneness, however. No, Jesus is much more bold. He asks for his followers to experience an incredible payoff in community. He requests no less than Trinity-level relationship!

When I (Russ) first was gripped with the nature of Jesus' prayer, I was forever changed. I had started exploring a move from practicing law to vocational ministry, because Senior Pastor Bill Hybels had invited me to become Willow Creek's director of small groups. Aside from the complications of such a transition, I was reluctant to turn over my life for something that held mere strategic leadership interest. I had been a Willow Creek elder long enough to see the impact of our transition to becoming a church of small groups. I could see that a small group foundation made sense in terms of good managerial practice. But I had never grappled with the deeper issues. Some elder, huh?

I began realizing that, unless I was fueled by a passion for community that transcended a wise church program, I could never leave my law practice. I prayed for God to endow me with a larger vision for small groups. Then I waited. No books helped me. Conversations with small groups gurus did little. One sleepless night, I sat in a Denny's restaurant (the only place open at 2:00 a.m. to tortured souls), and reread John 17. God answered my prayer with these words from the lips of Jesus: "So that they may be one as we are one."

These verses overwhelmed me with the implications for small group ministry. Jesus actually prayed that real people—this little band of real, live flawed followers—would find an amazing kind of oneness. That it's even possible for humans to find such relational connection is remarkable. Yet Jesus says it is available. You can request it!

Even more stunning, Jesus doesn't stop by requesting oneness for his inner circle. He shifts his focus to a broader audience: "My prayer is not for them alone. I pray also for those who will believe in me through their message, that all of them may be one, Father, just as you are in me and I am in you" (John 17:20–21). Jesus, on death row for our redemption, prayed a real prayer at a real place at a real time, not just for his followers, but for you, each person you know, each Christ-follower you are acquainted with in your church, every human being to believe in him. He prayed a prayer that they would find that same kind of oneness that he wanted for his followers, oneness that matched his experience in the Trinity.

## Decision Time

Now, *you* have to do something with that prayer. You can conclude that those were just flowery words, or that Jesus was in an emotional panic and didn't know what he was saying, but you have to do something with them. Can we conclude that he really meant what he prayed?

I did—so much so that I knew my best efforts and gifts would have to be put against the task of building a church of small groups, no matter what. I purposed that, until God clearly called otherwise, I had to be in on this mission. Ultimately it meant the sale of a law firm partnership, a move from the marketplace to vocational ministry, and a relearning of all new occupational skills. But I had to do something with the echo of Jesus' prayer and its implications for my church.

What does your church do with those words? Christ prayed for oneness among his immediate followers and those who would believe later. Is that the routine experience of your church? Probably not. Somehow churches have lost this vision. A cheapened theology has led to a cheapened doctrine of the church, a two-bit theology of community. Churches respond to Jesus' call with bargain-basement fellowship. We cannot settle for anything less than Jesus' dream of community. New visions, strategies, and tactics worthy of the theological model of oneness—these are not optional!

What if Jesus is describing a relational connection among mortal men and women that can only be explained theologically? The church can then join him in a grand vision of Christian friendship, unique from anything society can offer. We can refine our theology and be formed by our doctrine of God and the Trinity. The path to community is bound up in the person and identity of God himself.

Gilbert Bilezikian—one of Willow Creek's founders, Wheaton College professor emeritus, and our mentor on community—explains why the theological case for community is so important.

> This concern for the survival of the church down through the ages provides the explanation for the anguished tones of Jesus' prayer. He knew that if the church should fail to demonstrate community to the world, it would fail to accomplish its mission, because the world would have reason to disbelieve the gospel (vv. 21, 23). According to that prayer, the most convincing proof of the truth of the gospel is the perceptible oneness of his followers.[6]

In other words, only by understanding God's identity and nature can we experience the oneness he desires for his followers. God existed from and for all time, in and as community. God incarnate, by image and identity, led a life and ministry of radical relationship. Jesus knew, in fact, that only one standard could express the kind of friendship his followers should find in the community of faith—the standard of God's relational identity and Trinitarian nature.

If you allow yourself to embrace the full implications of Jesus' dream for community, it will grip your heart. It will motivate you to say, "I don't know what it's going to take to make that happen within a local church, but whatever it's going to take, we're going to wrestle through and figure it out." We have to rebuild biblical, theologically sound community as best we can. We must study, think, and plan ways for people to become spiritually mature through transformational relationships. Maybe, just maybe, real people in our day will begin to experience the kind of oneness God dreams they will find.

This is what God dreams for us and our churches. We are called to move into community, one at a time, on the basis of God's identity as Three in One. We cannot ignore his example in Christ's incarnation and parting prayer; these call every church to weave real community into the fabric of its life. We must find ways to answer that call by creating an expanding network of small groups. That is the theological case. The evidence is overwhelming. But it is just the beginning.

# Created for Community:
# The Sociological Evidence

*Christian brotherhood is not an ideal which we must realize; it is rather a reality created by God in Christ in which we may participate.*

DIETRICH BONHOEFFER, *LIFE TOGETHER*

We believe the theological evidence proves the case for building a church of small groups. But let's not stop there. There is equally compelling sociological evidence to show why every person and church needs true community. God created you to crave relationship. And it's in your best interest to embrace small group life.

## The Sociological Evidence: Who You Are

Like Dietrich Bonhoeffer, we believe that Christian brotherhood or unity is part of God's created order. This view of humanity applies to people at creation, after the Fall, and in our lives today. Not only are you God's image bearer, created for community, but you are also designed to seek God and enjoy interdependence with him, and to communally connect with and generate spiritual life in others.

### Designed for Dependence

The Bible reminds us that we as human beings are by nature dependent, that we cannot exist apart from the sustaining gift of life from God. Paul writes:

"He is the God who made the world and everything in it. Since
he is Lord of heaven and earth, he doesn't live in man-made temples,
and human hands can't serve his needs—for he has no needs. He himself gives life and breath to everything, and he satisfies every need
there is. From one man he created all the nations throughout the
whole earth. He decided beforehand which should rise and fall, and
he determined their boundaries." (Acts 17:24–26 NLT)

Then Paul delivers the punch line: "'His purpose in all of this was that the
nations should seek after God and perhaps feel their way toward him and
find him—though he is not far from any one of us'" (Acts 17:27 NLT).
God, the community-defined being, gives us life so that we will seek out
community with him. God wants relationship with us. And even when
we're not looking for God, God is always with us.

God himself doesn't need this connection with us. Yet, the Bible
repeatedly shows that he has chosen to be interdependent with us—that
is, to share our emotions, our decisions, our concerns, and our bodies.

Does it sound strange to say that God exposes his *emotions* to mere
mortals? While God met Moses atop Mount Sinai to give him the Ten
Commandments, the impatient Israelites built and worshiped a golden
calf. God became angry. "'I have seen these people,' the LORD said to
Moses, 'and they are a stiff-necked people. Now leave me alone so that
my anger may burn against them and that I may destroy them. Then I
will make you into a great nation'" (Exodus 32:9–10). Stunning but true:
God chooses emotional interdependence with fallible people like you and
me. You can "grieve the Holy Spirit of God" (Ephesians 4:30) as well as
give him "great delight" (Zephaniah 3:17).

God sometimes engages us in his *decisions*. When, for example, God
threatened to destroy sinful Sodom, the hometown of Abraham's nephew
Lot, Abraham pleaded: "Will you sweep away the righteous with the
wicked? What if there are fifty righteous people in the city? Will you really
sweep it away and not spare the place for the sake of the fifty righteous
people in it? Far be it from you to do such a thing—to kill the righteous
with the wicked" (Genesis 18:23–26). Abraham kept raising the stakes.
God remained surprisingly flexible, finally agreeing to spare Sodom and
Gomorrah for the sake of just ten righteous people.

But God doesn't simply wait for us to voice *concerns*. He engages with
us so deeply that he steps in when we cannot even identify the problem, let
alone venture a solution. Romans 8:26–27 says, "In the same way, the Spirit

helps us in our weakness. We do not know what we ought to pray for, but the Spirit himself intercedes for us with groans that words cannot express. And he who searches our hearts knows the mind of the Spirit, because the Spirit intercedes for the saints in accordance with God's will."

I (Russ) have always loved machinery—cars, motorcycles, anything with a motor. Every winter one of my three sons joins me in a great American male ritual: attending the Chicago Auto Show. While we drool at the new concept cars and dream of driving cars we'll never own, we're especially drawn to the latest technological advances. Ironically, despite my passion for engines, I am mechanically inept. So I particularly like the new computer diagnostic systems that search and monitor your car every time you start it and drive it.

If people can design such sophisticated monitors for cars, imagine the remarkable set of spiritual sensors activated in you by the indwelling work of the Holy Spirit. God's interest is so intense that "even the very hairs of your head are all numbered" (Matthew 10:30), and he counts all your tears (Psalm 56:8). Like the diagnostic system in a new car, the Holy Spirit monitors our deepest concerns. Then the Holy Spirit "greases the skids" of communication between us and God—to match our desires with God's perfect will.

Finally, God created us to house himself. Our real physical *bodies* double as his residences. That's why God cares so much what we do with our bodies: "Do you not know that your body is a temple of the Holy Spirit, who is in you, whom you have received from God? You are not your own; you were bought at a price. Therefore honor God with your body" (1 Corinthians 6:19–20).

## Designed for Interdependence

Just as God designed us to live in community with him, he designed us to be communal with and to reproduce spiritual life in others. This interdependence among humans is part of God's created order, not a consequence of the Fall:

> The LORD God said, "It is not good for the man to be alone. I will make a helper suitable for him."
>
> ... So the LORD God caused the man to fall into a deep sleep; and while he was sleeping, he took one of the man's ribs and closed up the place with flesh. Then the LORD God made a woman from the rib he had taken out of the man, and he brought her to the man.

The man said,

"This is now bone of my bones
    and flesh of my flesh;
she shall be called 'woman'
    for she was taken out of man."

For this reason a man will leave his father and mother and be united
to his wife, and they will become one flesh. (Genesis 2:18, 21–24)

God is One and yet Three, and Three who are yet One. God created
women and men for similar community, so that in a marriage two people
become one, yet the one couple is still two people. This creation order
survived the Fall, as Paul makes clear in his quotation of Genesis 2:24:
"In this same way, husbands ought to love their wives as their own bodies. He who loves his wife loves himself. . . 'For this reason a man will
leave his father and mother and be united to his wife, and the two will
become one flesh'" (Ephesians 5:28, 31).

Amazing, isn't it? God created us as separate individuals, yet made
us capable of being an inseparable part of another human being. This def-
inition of communal living applies to marriage; it also applies to the
church. Look again at Ephesians 5. Just as it is biblical for husbands to
love their wives as they love their own bodies, so also in the church: "After
all, no one ever hated his own body, but he feeds and cares for it, just as
Christ does the church—for we are members of his body" (Ephesians
5:29–30).

Paul makes an astonishing correlation. Just as God is Three in One
and marriage partners are two in one, so also in the church can separate
individuals become inseparable parts of Christ's body. Romans 12:4–5
agrees: "Just as each of us has one body with many members, and these
members do not all have the same function, so in Christ we who are many
form one body, and each member belongs to all the others."

This passage is often taught (rightly so) as a core text on diversity. In
verses 6–8, Paul explains why we need to identify, use, and respect our
individual gifts. But God intends us to use these gifts within the communion of saints. Once we enter the life of interdependence with God, we also
enter into communal life with each other. This is not a reality we can
choose against or ignore. It's the way God made us. Note how the early
believers "broke bread in their homes and ate together with glad and

sincere hearts" (Acts 2:46). How many churches understand fellowship as the communal expression of intimacy that God intends for us today?

Christians today know what the doctrine of humanity teaches about sin and depravity as well as about eternal grace and freedom through salvation. But unfortunately, our knowledge of the Bible has been shaped by the individualism of our culture, so that we teach the need for personal forgiveness—then stop. We neglect to preach the full doctrine of humanity, namely, that we are created to be dependent on God, to enjoy interdependence with God, and to experience communal interdependence within the church.

Why? Because we have not experienced the potential of our dependence on and interdependence with the triune God. We have missed out on the richness of communal living and do not know how to guide our churches toward God's vision.

As a result, today's church suffers from an "interdependence deficit," an affliction that is passed on from one generation to the next. After all, spiritual life is generational; it depends on one person passing the gospel message to another. Note Paul's words in Romans 10:14: "How, then, can they call on the one they have not believed in? And how can they believe in the one of whom they have not heard? And how can they hear without someone preaching to them?"

Paul also spoke of giving "birth" to a "son," Timothy (1 Timothy 1:2). While crediting Timothy's mother, Eunice, and grandmother, Lois, as physical and spiritual predecessors, Paul poured his life into Timothy. He instructed, "And the things you have heard me say in the presence of many witnesses entrust to reliable men who will also be qualified to teach others" (2 Timothy 2:2). Paul knew that each generation must pass on its faith and leadership to the next. Not only must we pass it on, we must be sure the person who receives the faith can teach someone else.

At Willow Creek, this is known as "being a Larry Clark." Larry Clark volunteered here for years. As a young man, he earned some money, but he cared more about investing himself in others, so he simplified his lifestyle to live on as little as possible. He even ate day-old food thrown out by local grocers so as to remain undistracted by the need to earn. Larry spent his time "giving birth to many sons."

He continued investing in people right up to our annual Small Group Leadership Retreat in 1999. At the weekend retreat, while Larry was on his morning run, a commuter bus struck and killed him. You cannot imagine the loss our church and many people in it suffered that day. But because Larry lived so dependent on God, interdependent with him and others, and invested in the next generation, countless people decided that day to be a Larry Clark. They learned from him that the only life worth living is one invested in generating the life of Christ in others.

We must rebuild an apologetic for *and practice of* community based on God's identity and dream for relational oneness. We can support this apologetic by a profound doctrine of humanity, founded on the truth of who God says we are. Then we can enter into the practice of building community and reproducing spiritual life.

## The Sociological Evidence: What You Need

So far we have presented theological and sociological evidence to demonstrate why congregations should move from being churches *with* small groups to becoming churches *of* small groups. Theologically, we've shown why God's communal nature requires you to respond by building community for yourself and your church. Sociologically, we've shown that you should accept the case for small groups because God created you to crave relationship.

We all know, however, that there's a big difference between knowing you should accept something and wanting to do it. We admit that we've based our case so far on God's terms. Now we'll switch to your terms. We'll show through the Bible and personal experience why it's in your best self-interest to embrace small group life.

The biblical record shows that true community offers four blessings:

- We get *strength* for life's storms.
- We receive *wisdom* for making important decisions.
- We experience *accountability,* which is vital to spiritual growth.
- We find *acceptance* that helps us repair our wounds.

The church is uniquely suited to offer these four blessings through a network of small groups. Such relationships become incredibly attractive to everyone they touch!

### Strength

Ecclesiastes 4:9–10 offers a practical reason for moving into community: "Two are better than one . . . if one falls down, his friend can help him up." Each individual can help the other carry a load too heavy to bear alone. Some of us go for years without experiencing major troubles, yet the Bible says trouble is a matter of "when," not "if." Jesus told his disciples, "In this world you will have trouble" (John 16:33).

I (Russ) learned that during Christmas of 1998. We began with our normal family activities—attending a Christmas Eve service, sharing dinner, opening gifts. Early on Christmas morning we climbed into our ten-year-old motor home for the long journey from Chicago to Phoenix. When you live in the frozen Midwest, the promise of better weather is reason enough to rise early on Christmas morning! As planned, my wife and I took turns driving well past nightfall. We stopped in northeast Texas for a quick refueling stop—quick, that is, for a gas-guzzling motor home. I took the wheel. My family fell asleep.

My lumbering motor home had nearly reached highway speed on the rural interstate when, suddenly, headlights shining into the dark winter night revealed a drunken woman dressed in black, walking down the middle of the highway. I tried swerving to miss her, but it was impossible. As I collided with her, her skull cracked the windshield, her body tore at the right side of the vehicle, and she was tossed into the ditch. I later learned she'd positioned herself on the road, hoping to commit suicide by being run over. She survived. I barely survived emotionally.

That senseless tragedy left me emotionally fragile, to a degree I couldn't have imagined. Recovery was long and difficult. Even driving felt dangerous. I had to rebuild a battered psyche and wasn't sure where to turn.

Yet that trauma gave me firsthand experience of God's promise that true community offers strength for life's storms. After the collision, I parked along the road, made a cellular 911 call, then nearly went into physical shock. Seconds later, I phoned a man in my small group, and my wife phoned a woman in hers. Within moments, two small groups—then the community surrounding those groups—began praying.

Their prayer support helped me begin the road to emotional recovery. My community listened during long conversations while I tried to process confusing emotions. When I wrestled with God—seeking to make sense of the experience—people offered reassurance and other help. I needed people to pray with and for me, and I came to know what it was to have someone "weep with those who weep" (Romans 12:15 NRSV). I experienced how the body of Christ can extend real, personal hands to someone in pain.

There will come a time when life turns against you, and you need help. The heroes of faith discovered this truth. David's friendship with Jonathan sustained him during Saul's persecution. On the run from Queen Jezebel, Elijah prayed that he might die; God led him to Elisha, an icon of fidelity. Naomi lost her husband and both sons, but she had Ruth to lean on. Without Priscilla and Aquila to save his life or Onesiphorus to encourage him, who knows how the apostle Paul might have endured persecution and imprisonment?

These heroes of faith survived adversity through faith and community. So can you. But you need to invest in community today, so you can reap the benefits during tomorrow's seasons of deprivation and loss. The Bible tells how to invest in community. James referred to God's command—"Love your neighbor as yourself" (Leviticus 19:18)—as "the royal law" (James 2:8). Paul advised, "Carry each other's burdens, and in this way you will fulfill the law of Christ" (Galatians 6:2).

## Wisdom

Small groups also provide wisdom when we face important decisions. As Proverbs 15:22 explains, "Plans fail for lack of counsel, but with many advisors they succeed." The more advisors you have, God says, the more likely you are to make right choices.

In this era of corporate downsizing, you probably know people who have lost their jobs. You can easily imagine what has become an all-too-common scenario: you hear rumors of financial trouble; your boss calls you in for a closed-door conversation; she tells you your department has been eliminated; security escorts you to your office. Suddenly you are without a paycheck, job title, familiar routine, or workplace social network.

Or perhaps you've had trouble parenting—or know someone dealing with difficult children. Smart and loving parents pour their lives into their children, yet sometimes things go wrong. Raising children is especially challenging for single parents. Can you picture how trusted members of a small group might help people sort through complex choices to find a job or heal their families?

My small group has helped me make major decisions. As mentioned in chapter 1, in the mid-1990s, I (Russ) had a law practice and was an elder at Willow Creek Community Church. One day Senior Pastor Bill Hybels asked for an appointment. I expected we'd talk about elder matters. But Bill turned my world upside down. He challenged me to leave my law firm and become Willow Creek's full-time leader of small group ministry.

I gathered my small group and other friends around me, submitting my thinking and ultimate decisions to them. They cross-examined me like lawyers, balancing varied issues and concerns, providing a treasure trove of insight. They gave me a confidence I wouldn't have had if I'd made my decision alone. Without my advisors, I might have chosen a path to personal and family disaster.

## Accountability

The Bible presents yet another piece of sociological evidence for community. It says that we need friends to hold us accountable and offer acceptance while we change.

Friendships can provide unique opportunities for spiritual growth, especially when we covenant to be mutually vulnerable and tell the truth. Most of us really want to become more like Christ. We read the Bible to gain insight into ourselves. But James describes how even that strategy fails when we avoid true community: "For if you just listen and don't obey, it is like looking at your face in a mirror but doing nothing to improve your appearance. You see yourself, walk away, and forget what you look like. But if you keep looking steadily into God's perfect law—the law that sets you free—and if you do what it says and don't forget what you heard, then God will bless you for doing it." (James 1:23–25 NLT).

You've probably experienced this simple dynamic yourself or seen it in others. Typical believers get something out of reading the Bible or hearing a sermon. These messages help them spot spiritual hygiene problems. But messages function as mirrors; they reflect your image only while you look at them. Turn away, and you can ignore the reflection.

If you receive something from God's Word or a sermon and then open up to trusted sisters or brothers, you will find that those friends can act as permanent mirrors. They will hold you accountable to keep your eyes on the reflection God revealed—even when you'd rather turn away.

Before we can connect with each other, we must overcome our fear of self-disclosure. The best way for healthy small groups to invite each other into accountability is to formulate a written covenant. Members commit to meeting times, group goals, and confidentiality. People need to know that their secrets will stay inside the group. Only then will they feel safe enough to share what they see in God's mirror of truth—or loved enough to invite others to help them change and grow.

Proverbs 27:17 reminds us why we need fellowship for true spiritual growth: "As iron sharpens iron, a friend sharpens a friend" (NLT).

Such sharpening, a rare gift of life change, won't happen unless we get close to each other. Small groups offer a connection—between Jesus, others, and ourselves—that purifies us. As John explains, "But if we walk in the light, as he is in the light, we have fellowship with one another, and the blood of Jesus, his Son, purifies us from all sin" (1 John 1:7).

## Acceptance

We need community to achieve lasting transformation. But during this change we also need acceptance and care, something that, more than any other institution, the church is uniquely suited to offer—especially through a network of small groups. Does this claim sound inflated? Consider the competition.

When you talk with people about their families, you'll discover a startling truth few want to admit. Many people experience more pain than love and acceptance in their families. Divorce, substance abuse, spousal and sexual abuse, overwork, and financial stress contort family dynamics. If this isn't true for you, then stop right now and thank God!

Nor can people depend on their workplaces for acceptance and care. The days of lifelong job security are over, replaced by global competition, downsizing, and workplace violence. Every technological change creates new jobs but eliminates old ones. Simply trying to survive at work requires so much energy that few people have time for deep friendship with colleagues.

You can't depend on your neighborhood for acceptance and care either. Sure, some people are blessed with great neighbors. But most people are too busy working or fulfilling family responsibilities to make friends next door. And whether they live on less prosperous streets or in gated communities, almost everyone fears violence from strangers.

Though most people have become resigned to isolation, no longer expecting to find true community, the church can offer ultimate friendship. It is the only institution given this mandate from Jesus: "My command is this: Love each other as I have loved you. Greater love has no one than this, that he lay down his life for his friends" (John 15:12–13). Jesus really does expect us to lay down whatever we have, however we need to, whenever requested.

Is your church living up to its Christ-mandated potential for community? You already know that the church can't compete with other institutions in terms of entertainment value. When Willow Creek Community Church opened its doors in 1975, seekers were impressed with our innovative use of video, drama, contemporary music, and good sound and lighting. We still aim to offer relevant communication. But our services will never match the latest cinematic special effects, amusement attractions, music and video innovations, or computer games.

Where can the church compete? In community! We all know that churches sometimes experience frustrating conflicts, but consider what society offers to people who seek relationship—bars, bowling, and bingo. The church is the only place where most people, whether introvert or extrovert, have a reasonable promise of finding healthy, functional, accepting relationships.

■

The sociological evidence is in: All the benefits of community are yours—especially if you teach that God created us to crave relationship and then organize your church so people can connect. As your small group strategies mature, people will find the kind of friends who stick "closer than a brother" (Proverbs 18:24). They'll find and offer comfort, wisdom, and the accountability that produces spiritual growth.

Have the theological and sociological evidence persuaded you to pursue this winsome vision? If not, then consider the organizational evidence for why your congregation should become a church of small groups.

# What the Church Needs to Grow: The Organizational Evidence

*Forty years ago a revolution began in the church....After centuries of institutionalization the church is returning to the homes and lives of its people....Small group ministry is sweeping the church and writing another chapter in its rich heritage. By God's grace, and by applying God's wisdom, your congregation can benefit from and contribute to this revolution.*

JEFF ARNOLD, *STARTING SMALL GROUPS*

We've shown that God created us to crave relationship, with himself and each other. We've looked at the benefits you'll find in true community. Now it's time to translate a vision for community into the day-to-day reality of local church life. Our final argument—the organizational evidence—will prove why congregations should move from being churches *with* small groups to becoming churches *of* small groups.

The organizational evidence depends on two principles. First, your church will best meet each member's needs by honoring what Carl George defines as "span of care." This principle ensures that everybody is cared for, but no one cares for too many people. Second, the church cannot function as God intends unless people see themselves as members of one body. Each part must take responsibility so that Christ's body can do its work in the world. Only when everyone works together will each life be transformed.

## Span of Care

No other strategy will revolutionize a church of small groups as the span of care strategy does. Carl George describes this revolution in his book *Nine Keys to Effective Small Group Leadership*:

I have become convinced that God is leading many churches in a quiet revolution. This transformation or change is significant because it is allowing Spirit-filled, God-gifted people to focus on loving one another, speaking the truth in love, and releasing additional leaders who can multiply the reformation elsewhere. The consequences are that many, many people are being provoked to love and good works through healthy, reproductive small groups. To a certain extent, even the foundations of our society are being rebuilt through this lay-driven movement.[1]

## Everyone Needs Connection

Willow Creek Community Church discovered the need for span of care the hard way. Our founders drove home the vision and values of relationship, and our membership grew phenomenally. Yet, after fifteen years as a church, we realized that we weren't giving every person the chance to experience transforming relationship. Needs were neglected. People lost the ability to build up the church and its people.

I (Bill) remember how hard our church tried to connect people during the early years of our new small group adventure. We had spent a year building small groups as a "pilot ministry." We were still experimenting, wondering whether these groups made a difference. So we took a survey.

The results were shocking, in a positive way. Of all the people we surveyed, over five hundred said that they had been thinking of leaving Willow Creek, but decided to stay—because they were now connected to a small group. What a bell ringer! These five hundred people remained members because they were invited into a small group community. Their lives were being transformed. These amazing survey results convinced us that to truly connect people to Jesus Christ and one another, we had to build life-changing small groups. And we had to give everyone a shot at community.

Reorganizing your congregation into a church of small groups is hard work. You need to present the organizational case to every segment of your church, including your ministries to children and adults, couples and singles, men and women, jocks and computer geeks, the mature and the emotionally unstable, the leaders and newly converted. But span of care can help your church achieve reorganization.

## No One Can Do It All

Span of care means breaking large, complex groups into smaller, more manageable units, then assigning leaders to each span of care—so that everyone's needs are met. We first encounter this historic pattern for leadership and communal connection in Exodus 18. Until his father-in-law, Jethro, paid him a visit, Moses believed what many Christians do: "If you want something done right, you had better do it yourself."

Moses stood up to Pharoah, led Israel out of Egypt, talked with God on Mount Sinai, asked God to provide pure water and daily food—and wore himself out. Scholars estimate that, all by himself, Moses was trying to lead a nation of at least two million followers.[2] He didn't even have the support of his wife and two sons, because he'd left them with Jethro when God spoke from the burning bush and sent him to Egypt.

According to Exodus 18, having heard how God had helped Moses bring Israel out of Egypt, Jethro reunited Moses with his wife and sons. Jethro and Moses caught up on their news, and the older man said he was "delighted to hear about all the good things the LORD had done for Israel" (Exodus 18:9).

The next day he watched Moses handle disputes from morning till evening. As priest of Midian and owner of a large sheep flock, Jethro had some management experience. So he asked Moses:

> "What is this you are doing for the people? Why do you alone sit as judge, while all these people stand around you from morning till evening?"
>
> Moses answered him, "Because the people come to me to seek God's will. Whenever they have a dispute, it is brought to me, and I decide between the parties and inform them of God's decrees and laws." (Exodus 18:14–16)

Anyone who has tried to manage people in business, politics, or the church can sympathize with Moses. His leadership style wasn't working, but he was far too busy to look for a better strategy. Fortunately, Jethro was wise enough to offer a solution:

> "What you are doing is not good. You and these people who come to you will only wear yourselves out. The work is too heavy for you; you cannot handle it alone. Listen now to me and I will give you some advice, and may God be with you. You must be the people's representative before God and bring their disputes to him. Teach them the decrees and laws, and show them the way to live and the duties they are to perform. But select capable men from all the people—men who fear God, trustworthy men who hate dishonest gain—and appoint

them as officials over thousands, hundreds, fifties and tens. Have them serve as judges for the people at all times, but have them bring every difficult case to you; the simple cases they can decide themselves. That will make your load lighter, because they will share it with you." (Exodus 18:17–22)

Do the math and you'll see that Jethro's recommended span of care was five to ten people per leader. One person could shepherd ten people. Someone else could care for the leaders of five or ten units. Another leader could oversee leaders at the "thousands" level.

The Bible gives several more examples of God's interest in organizational integrity. The prophet Jeremiah condemned King Jehoiachin for neglecting the people under his care: "'Because you have scattered my flock and driven them away and have not bestowed care on them, I will bestow punishment on you for the evil you have done,' declares the LORD" (Jeremiah 23:2).

Jesus came to reach the world but focused his ministry on twelve disciples. They began a church that, after Pentecost, exploded into a body of over three thousand people. But soon a problem arose. "The Grecian Jews among them complained against the Hebraic Jews because their widows were being overlooked in the daily distribution of food" (Acts 6:1). So the Twelve asked the group to appoint seven deacons, thus freeing the apostles to preach.

As the apostles planted new churches across Asia Minor, they followed the span of care principle. Paul, for example, instructed Timothy and Titus: "Straighten out what was left unfinished and appoint elders in every town" (Titus 1:5).

For span of care to work, leaders like Moses, Old Testament kings, Jesus, and the apostle Paul needed to carve up the workload, then identify which leaders would serve best at which levels. Likewise, when a church adopts span of care by creating a small group infrastructure, needs get met and leaders remain effective. No one person tries to do it all.

Even before I (Russ) began directing Willow Creek's small groups ministry, I saw the span of care principle at work. I was helping a couple revise their will. As a paralegal modified the documents, the husband and wife took turns telling me about their dilemma at church. They'd been leading a small group that had lost all its members to corporate transfers and other moves. The husband had recently changed jobs, and the couple had two demanding infants. Given the stress in their lives, they were wondering whether they should lead a new small group. Then they said, "But we can't imagine *not* continuing to lead, because we'd miss the care we receive from our coach." ("Coach" is Willow Creek's term for a leader of small group leaders.)

They wanted to stay in the leadership game in order to continue receiving care. This was our dream come true: nobody had to care for too many; everyone was getting cared for. We at Willow Creek had no way to achieve this level of care until we put span of care to work by organizing everyone into small groups. We designated leaders to care for groups of children, women, men, couples, and families. Coaches care for leaders, and coaches receive care from staff leaders.

We admit that needs sometimes still go unmet. But we are narrowing the gap between needs and care. People look on small groups as families that offer support in crisis, wisdom for decisions, mirrors of truth, and true acceptance. Finally, our church is organizationally positioned to care for every person who comes to us, and, more often than not, we get it right when needs arise.

## Members of One Body

The span-of-care principle explains how small groups help a church to meet everyone's individual needs. The members-of-one-body principle addresses individual responsibility. Because we are members of one body, each with a part to play, the church cannot become what Christ intends unless each member accepts responsibility. As everyone works together, God transforms individual lives, creating the kind of oneness experienced in the Trinity, the kind of community Christ dreams of for us. Small groups offer the best way for everyone to play a part and become transformed through working together.

### Each Part Must Do Its Work

For the church to be the church, each person must participate. The reason, as Paul explains in 1 Corinthians 12:12–13, is that God sees us as members of one body: "The body is a unit, though it is made up of many parts; and though all its parts are many, they form one body. So it is with Christ. For we were all baptized by one Spirit into one body—whether Jews or Greeks, slave or free—and we were all given the one Spirit to drink."

In verses 14 through 27, Paul describes the absurdity of Christians viewing themselves as individuals related only to Christ, not to each other.

Unless each person accepts responsibility and treats the other parts with respect, the whole body suffers:

> Now the body is not made up of one part but of many. If the foot should say, "Because I am not a hand, I do not belong to the body," it would not for that reason cease to be part of the body. And if the ear should say, "Because I am not an eye, I do not belong to the body," it would not for that reason cease to be part of the body. If the whole body were an eye, where would the sense of hearing be? If the whole body were an ear, where would the sense of smell be? But in fact God has arranged the parts in the body, every one of them, just as he wanted them to be. If they were all one part, where would the body be? As it is, there are many parts, but one body.
>
> The eye cannot say to the hand, "I don't need you!" And the head cannot say to the feet, "I don't need you!" On the contrary, those parts of the body that seem to be weaker are indispensable, and the parts that we think are less honorable we treat with special honor. And the parts that are unpresentable are treated with special modesty, while our presentable parts need no special treatment. But God has combined the members of the body and has given greater honor to the parts that lacked it, so that there should be no division in the body, but that its parts should have equal concern for each other. If one part suffers, every part suffers with it; if one part is honored, every part rejoices with it.
>
> Now you are the body of Christ, and each one of you is a part of it.

Before and after this description of Christ's church as members of one body, Paul describes various spiritual gifts, each "given for the common good" (1 Corinthians 12:7). When each part of the body does its work, spiritual gifts can have a massive impact on church ministry. When each member accepts responsibility, then the church can do Christ's work in the world. Small groups offer the best way for people to accept responsibility, treat others with respect, and thus experience being members of one body.

## The Beauty of the Whole

In Ephesians 4 Paul argues that the church cannot function as Christ intends unless it works as a body. As everyone works together toward unity, harnessing their gifts to the common good, individual members experience transformed lives:

> Make every effort to keep the unity of the Spirit through the bond of peace. There is one body and one Spirit—just as you were called to one hope when you were called—one Lord, one faith, one baptism; one God and Father of all, who is over all and through all and in all.
>
> But to each one of us grace has been given as Christ apportioned it. . . . It was he who gave some to be apostles, some to be prophets, some to be evangelists, and some to be pastors and teachers, to prepare God's people for works of service, so that the body of Christ may be built up until we all reach unity in the faith and in the knowledge of the Son of God and become mature, attaining to the whole measure of the fullness of Christ.
>
> Then we will no longer be infants, tossed back and forth by the waves, and blown here and there by every wind of teaching and by the cunning and craftiness of men in their deceitful scheming. Instead, speaking the truth in love, we will in all things grow up into him who is the Head, that is, Christ. From him the whole body, joined and held together by every supporting ligament, grows and builds itself up in love, as each part does its work. (Ephesians 4:3–7, 11–16)

I (Russ) have belonged to ten churches during my forty-three years and have yet to find a church that truly lives the Ephesians 4:16 ideal of everyone doing their part. But having seen countless church organizational designs, I can tell you this: sizzling services, extra ministry programs, or new curricula will not transform yours into a church where people really do build each other up in love, "as each part does its work."

The churches that come closest to this ideal all share a common vision and practice. Their leaders—senior pastor, staff, elders, key volunteers—are bold enough to imagine the seemingly impossible. They believe the church can experience oneness by transforming people through community. And these leaders have recognized that small groups are the key, the common practice, for realizing their vision. They have taken action.

These church leaders have chosen small groups because they know it's the only way for each member to experience the power of transforming relationships. They want to become churches colored by the vibrant community and loving interdependence God longs to see in his bride.

They know that working the small group pattern into their fabric of church life is the only way they can become a true body—joined and held together by each supporting ligament, building itself up in love, as each part does its work.

## What Is Your Verdict?

The trial isn't over till the jury or judge renders a verdict. If I (Russ) was back in the courtroom, I might use this closing argument to finalize my case for building a church of small groups: "Ladies and gentleman of the jury, the case for small groups is now complete. As I said at the beginning, yours is an awesome responsibility. God has put the verdict in your hands, trusting you to review the evidence, soberly and objectively. You must determine how you view the evidence for yourselves and your church.

"We began with the theological reality that God's communal nature, Three persons in One, requires you to respond by building community for yourself and for your church. We explained your God-created sociological need for relationship, a need best met through small group life. Finally, we argued that unless your church organizes itself to meet each person's need for relationship and provides a way for each person to take part, you will never come close to God's plan for community.

"We have presented clear and convincing proof for building a church of small groups. You may choose to reject authoritative evidence from Scripture or find that this evidence is irrelevant to your decision. You may even fail to render your verdict completely—by leaving it as theory rather than a reality that reshapes your church. But you do have the verdict in your hands. We pray you will decide fully in favor of building a church of small groups."

# PURSUING COMMUNITY IN SMALL GROUPS

Part 2

When I (Bill) was in seminary, I needed to buy a car. My car was almost dead, and I had little money (a prerequisite for seminary students), so I headed to a used car dealer. I was young and naive and had never purchased a car from a dealer, only from my brother. The used car salesman sized me up in thirty seconds. "Ever bought a car before?" he asked.

"No," I replied.

"Do you know exactly what you are looking for?"

I shrugged. "Well, not really."

He asked, "Are you trading in your car?"

Without thinking, I said, "Yes!" not knowing he was adding my trade-in value to the price of cars he was about to show me.

The salesman began to drool. I was a T-bone steak, and he was a hungry wolf. "I will take care of you," he said, with a Texas-sized grin. And you know what? He did take care of me. Before I knew it, I was signing papers and heading out the door with a nice blue sedan only four years old, with shiny tires, power everything, and a full tank of gas. It was a great day . . . or so I thought.

In my haste to make a deal, I had taken a brief test drive, walked around the car, and kicked the tires—as they do on TV. I knew this salesman had sold cars to other seminary students, so I assumed he was one of those "I love Jesus, the church, and church leaders, so I always tell the truth and give up-and-coming pastors a great deal" guys. Wrong. Instead, he was Mr. "I prey on seminary students, because they are broke, new in town, and don't know a dead car from a Dead Sea scroll." We cut the deal so fast that I made a classic first-time buyer mistake—I never looked under the hood. And he was not eager to show me "what lies beneath."

Within four months I had to spend another $2,500 for a transmission, alternator, fuel pump, and other gadgets that have no real function but cost "$150 plus labor." It was a hard lesson. Since then I've never bought a car without looking under the hood and having a mechanic check it, too. That rule has served us well.

"What makes a small group work?" This is a question we hear often. People want to know what it looks like when a group really acts like a little community. Pastors and church leaders thinking about moving toward a church of groups sometimes wonder, "What is really under the hood?" They have heard great stories about small groups and changed lives, but is it all hype? Others believe in groups and what they can do but haven't had a chance to "look inside" and discover what it takes to pursue oneness in a small group community.

What are the foundational or core components of small group community, and how do they contribute to church life? From studying the Acts 2 church and observing small groups at Willow Creek and other churches, we have identified four nonnegotiables for achieving spiritual community within small groups. Omitting even one of these essential elements will severely reduce your church's community quotient:

1. Small groups are built on authentic relationships (see chapter 4).
2. Small groups are places where truth meets life (see chapter 5).
3. Small groups experience healthy conflict (see chapter 6).
4. Small groups provide well-balanced shepherding, so that people are both cared for and discipled (see chapter 7).

With these four components in place you will begin to build the kind of group life that you will want to reproduce throughout the church. So let's "lift the hood" and take a close look at what groups can really be like when they are functioning well.

# Small Groups Are Built on Authentic Relationships

*Small groups are microcosms of God's creation community. Wherever two or more persons come together, they become an actual reflection of the image and likeness of God. Small groups are the basic arena for either imaging the redeeming presence of God or projecting destructive human systems. Every small or large gathering of humanity exists in this tension of manifesting an inhuman structure or embodying divinely redemptive relationships.*

GARETH ICENOGLE, *BIBLICAL FOUNDATIONS FOR SMALL GROUP MINISTRY*

If you have followed Christian counselor Larry Crabb's writings, you have probably been impressed by his search for spiritual community and personal growth. In his book *The Safest Place on Earth* he pleads with readers to return to authentic spiritual community with Christ and others. Crabb knows small groups play a part in this return. He is equally aware that small group practices and values must change to achieve spiritual community.

Citing the frustration many group advocates feel, Crabb writes, "One small group pastor said to me over lunch, 'We've got to move to another level. Good things are happening in our groups, but not what most needs to happen, not what I somehow know could happen. We arrange our bodies in a circle, but our souls are sitting in straight-backed chairs facing away from the others.'"[1]

That last comment captures a haunting reality far too familiar among pastors and group leaders. *Bodies in a circle, souls turned away.* If you've tried to navigate the seas of spiritual community, those words slam against your soul like storm waves against the hull of a weary ship. *Bodies in a circle, souls turned away.*

Do you wonder whether small group life really can yield the fruits of transformation and relational integrity? What does it take for small groups to get it right, to set aside pretense and join one another in meaningful, Spirit-empowered ways? Must small group life remain business as usual? *Bodies in a circle, souls turned away?*

## Growing in Community: The Irreducible Minimum

There is no fast food at the table of community. Americans are trained to want it all—right now. A recent diet program promises you will lose ten pounds in forty-eight hours. I'm afraid to ask how. It reminds me of a joke my mother told when I was shedding pounds for the wrestling team. "Bill, want an easy way to lose ten pounds of ugly fat?"

"Sure, Mom! What do I do?" I asked.

She smirked. "Cut off your head!"

I wanted results without work. And Christians want change without challenge, strength without suffering, community without commitment.

Spiritual transformation—one of the great purposes of community building—requires what Eugene Peterson calls "a long obedience in the same direction." The apostle Paul put it this way:

> I want to know Christ and the power of his resurrection and the fellowship of sharing in his sufferings, becoming like him in his death, and so, somehow, to attain to the resurrection from the dead.
>
> ... I press on to take hold of that for which Christ Jesus took hold of me. ... Forgetting what is behind and straining toward what is ahead, I press on toward the goal to win the prize for which God has called me heavenward in Christ Jesus. (Philippians 3:10–14)

Notice Paul's intention. He knew, as Teaching Pastor John Ortberg reminds us at Willow Creek, that no one drifts into spiritual transformation. It requires effort. Like Paul, Peter also understood the need to pursue growth:

> So *make every effort* to apply the benefits of these promises to your life. Then your faith will produce a life of moral excellence. A life of

moral excellence leads to knowing God better. Knowing God leads to self-control. Self-control leads to *patient endurance*, and *patient endurance* leads to godliness. Godliness leads to love for other Christians, and finally you will grow to have genuine love for everyone. So, dear brothers and sisters, *work hard* to prove that you really are among those God has called and chosen. Doing this, you will never stumble or fall away. And God will open wide the gates of heaven for you to enter into the eternal Kingdom of our Lord and Savior Jesus Christ. (2 Peter 1:5–7, 10–11 NLT; emphasis ours)

You cannot pursue a life of transformation—sanctification in Bible terms—on your own. Peter says it is a progression that culminates in genuine love expressed in community! One of the great payoffs for your own spiritual growth is the impact it has on the community of Christ-followers. Personal prayer, Scripture reading and memorizing, solitude, and other spiritual practices are essential, but pursued apart from community they fall short in producing the degree of transformation Christ intends. Spiritual growth cannot take place apart from community, and the fruit of such growth can only be expressed in community. Christlikeness is relational to the core. We must turn our souls toward one another and become what Dietrich Bonhoeffer calls "bringers of the message of salvation" to one another.

But the practical question is, "How?" How do we work out our salvation together in an environment of community? How do we enter into the "divinely redemptive relationships" that Icenogle described in this chapter's opening?

Christian leaders have used similar language to describe what small groups must do to build authentic relationships. Henri Nouwen encouraged believers to become people "who know and are known, who care and are cared for, who forgive and are being forgiven, who love and are being loved."[2] Parker Palmer, in *To Know As We Are Known: Education As a Spiritual Journey*, called educators to practice a knowledge centered on love and the true knowing of students in the context of community. In a four-week series on community, Bill Hybels preached on knowing and being known, serving and being served, loving and being loved, and celebrating and being celebrated.

We tested our description for authentic relationships within the laboratory of Willow Creek's 2,700 small groups. Time and again, whether we were dealing with task groups, recovery groups, or men's ministry, we discovered that five practices are absolutely necessary for any group to build authentic relationships: self-disclosure, care giving, humility, truth-telling, and affirmation.

## Self-Disclosure: To Know and Be Known

To known and be known, we must first understand intimacy, then overcome barriers to intimacy by exercising appropriate self-disclosure. Deep down, we all want people to know who we are—to care about our story, our pain, and our dreams. Yet most of us would rather talk about ourselves than try hard to know others. Friends who ask questions and really listen are like water to a parched throat. No group, friendship, or marriage will achieve intimacy unless people seek both to know and be known. Julie Gorman, a Fuller Seminary professor and small group advocate, writes:

> True community is more than being together. A person does not develop trust in others simply by being in a group where members study together, pray together, and share a common group leader. Trust involves relatedness. Relatedness is more than presence although that is the beginning. To relate, one must know, and to know one must work at being open to trust.[3]

Perhaps the great barometer of true and loving relationships is the grief experienced when they end. To build true intimacy or community requires love; to lose it demands grief. Jesus wept when Lazarus died (John 11); the Ephesian elders mourned Paul's departure (Acts 20). Lyman Coleman, founder of Serendipity Ministries and a champion for small groups worldwide, recently lost his beloved wife, Margaret. If indeed grief is a measure of a relationship's depth, then the letter Lyman sent to his associates is a testimony to intimacy. Here, with permission, are excerpts:

> She was an original—totally unpredictable, mischievous, outrageous with a dash of proper English reserve, and a wicked sense of humor. She was also deeply, deeply spiritual. Margaret loved people. Reading to children. Walking in the woods "scrunching" the leaves. Garage sales. Dressing up for Halloween as a "bag lady." High tea with crumpets. Pinching the cheeks of new babies. Smelling a new book. Crazy hats and unusual walking sticks. She hated bad gram-

mar, fancy clothes, and pretense of any sort. Her idea of a good night was popcorn by the fireside with a few friends who could talk intelligently about C. S. Lewis and leave early. As I deal with my own grief, I need to distinguish between grief which I am experiencing now, and mourning, which I will do for the rest of my life. My grief has to do with loss, loneliness, anger, helplessness and spiritual emptiness. In time, I trust this will pass. My mourning for Margaret will never pass. It is the piece where I will recall, relive and celebrate the fabulous years that we shared together.

The most painful decision of my life was asking God to take her home. She had been suffering from repeated brain seizures and her body was wasted. I whispered in her ear, "Honey, I love you. I love you. Jesus wants you to come home. We are going to be alright. We give you permission to let go." She closed her eyes and fell asleep.

Lyman finishes the letter with these heavy, yet hope-filled words:

As I write this letter, I realize I am without my editor. My greatest critic. My teammate. Soulmate. Prayermate. Partner in everything. We traveled the roads less traveled together in hard times and good times. Honey, I miss you. I miss you. I miss you. I will keep the light on for the kids. I will be there for friends. And one day, we are going to join you. All of us. Because Jesus promised it. "Precious in the sight of the Lord is the death of his saints" (Psalm 116:15).

Why do we desire and even expect such intimacy in marriage while in the church we sacrifice authentic community on the altar of casual camaraderie? Why do we erect barriers to intimacy and settle for surface friendships? Building a church filled with little communities—a church of groups—requires us to name those barriers. As one man said, "In order to see, I have to be willing to be seen. If a man takes off his sunglasses, I can hear him better." Knowing and being known means dismantling surface barriers (sunglasses) as well as deeper defenses, such as fear, shame, pride, and laziness. In *Equipping the Saints*, Christine M. Anderson explains that removing barriers to intimacy means rejecting self-sufficiency and disposable relationships, wanting more than "what Cornel West calls a 'hotel society.' In such a society, one may live in the company of others, but the connections are tenaciously superficial and unrelentingly transitory."[4]

To allow others to see deeply into our lives is the greatest gift we can ever give them. It is a gift wrapped in trust, hope, and love. Groups achieve this gift of self through appropriate self-disclosure. We tell our story and give people a window into our souls. You can find practical self-disclosure and community-building exercises in *201 Questions* by Jerry Jones, *Icebreakers* by Serendipity, and *Leading Life-Changing Small Groups* by Bill Donahue.

These exercises foster a deeper knowing, one rooted in love. As Parker Palmer emphasizes in *To Know As We Are Known*, knowing doesn't always equal love. He cautions against pursuing knowledge of others simply out of curiosity, "an amoral passion," or desire for control. Rather, he counsels us to pursue "knowledge that originates ... in compassion, or love—a source celebrated not in our intellectual tradition but in our spiritual heritage.... In such knowing we know and are known as members of one community, and our knowing becomes a way of reweaving that community's bonds."[5]

If you can't hear the sound of church bells in that last sentence you need a hearing aid. At Willow Creek, we can no longer imagine the local church apart from group life, because it is within our small groups that each person is grafted into the community of love that Christ died to redeem. You cannot reweave the bonds of community in your church—offering every member the gift of knowing and being known—apart from a small group structure. Authentic relationship is a nonnegotiable in creating biblical community, and self-disclosure is the first step.

## Care Giving: To Love and Be Loved

As we move to deeper levels of knowing each other, we learn how to love and be loved. Jesus says, "The greatest love is shown when people lay down their lives for their friends" (John 15:13 NLT). In his first letter, John gives this example of laying down our lives for others: "But if one of you has enough money to live well, and sees a brother or sister in need and refuses to help—how can God's love be in that person?" (1 John 3:17 NLT).

This bold, compassionate, life-giving, 1 Corinthians 13 kind of love begins with listening and remembering. I (Bill) am still working on this "love others first" orientation. But it was profoundly lacking in my first associate pastorate, where I oversaw Christian education, evangelism, and youth. I also did basic counseling and some pulpit teaching—all while finishing seminary! I moved quickly and decisively, far too busy to lay aside my to-do list, let alone my life, for the benefit of others. I used no spiritual gift assessments, no personality profiles. I gave some personal attention to youth, but simply filled adults into slots. My motto was, "We have a need, you have a pulse, so we have a match!" I prayed they had no real needs. Years later, I wonder whether those folks might have described my shepherding with this parody of Psalm 23:

> *Bill is my pastor, I do not want!*
> *He leadeth me to junior high sleepovers,*
> *He ignoreth my soul.*
> *He maketh me do door-to-door evangelism for his job's sake.*
> *Though I walk incessantly up and down the aisles of the church,*
> *you are not with me. Your wife and your staff, they run from me.*
> *You leadeth me to the missionary banquet; you fill me with a*
> *potluck dinner, my soft drink overflows.*
> *Surely the stewardship committee will follow me all the days of my*
> *life! And I will dwell in the children's nursery forever.*

When I phoned, I wonder if they said to themselves, "Oh, good, it's Bill, my shepherd who loves and cares about me," or rather, "What does he want now?"

Loving requires active listening and thoughtful remembering, especially in a small group relationship. Really listening sounds like, "Wow! I couldn't help but pick up your joy when you said that! That made your day, didn't it!" It goes beyond what is shared because you really do care. "Tell me more about that. I really want to understand." Active listening honors others, expresses love, and puts Scripture into action. "Everyone should be quick to listen, slow to speak, and slow to become angry" (James 1:19). James wants us to put people first, because people matter to God.

Active listening flows into thoughtful remembering. Sending a thank you note, reminding someone you're praying for them, embracing them after church, offering a simple gift or encouraging e-mail or phone message—these simple gestures shout, "I remember!" Taken together, these small expressions of caring love create an environment that invites relational integrity and spiritual transformation.

Remembering also means acting as "living reminders of Jesus Christ."[6] Those who do pastoral ministry—pastors and small group leaders—are healing reminders who help people remember the wounds of the past, connecting them to the healing Christ and the healing community.

We are sustaining reminders who help others draw nurture and strength from Jesus Christ. And we are guiding reminders who provide spiritual direction by confronting and inspiring. In all these ways we not only remember our people, but we help them remember the work of the ever-present Christ in the new community.

Combine this kind of loving with a knowing that connects small group members in deep relationship, and you have the beginnings of authentic community. The knowing and loving quotient in your group will be the evidence of authentic relationships. To merely connect and not know fosters the veneer of sociability; to know and not to love produces only collegial familiarity.

There is another ingredient to add to the relational mix: humility that stems from serving one another.

## Humility: To Serve and Be Served

A Christian leader who is not willing to serve is not fit to lead. But it is amazing how often we fall prey to conventional wisdom instead of biblical practices. Serving others may sometimes go unnoticed. But *not* serving others stands out like a sore thumb. While helping set up for an event, some church members said of a pastoral staff member, "You won't see him lift a finger when it involves anything but teaching. Remember when we needed help moving those chairs? He just stood there sipping his coffee. Maybe it was *below* him. I guess he just doesn't do chairs."

I wonder if that is our attitude as leaders. "I don't do chairs." Like the cleaning people who "don't do windows," we are apt to select only serving options that we enjoy or benefit from. Not Jesus. Jesus would do chairs. Actually, Jesus did feet. We are not real good at doing feet. But Jesus put on the towel, grabbed the basin, and did feet. John writes, "He now showed them the full extent of his love" (John 13:1). Certainly this comment refers ultimately to the cross, but undoubtedly it includes the humble act of service. For Jesus it was an act of supreme humble love.

Such devotion to service is not prized by trial lawyers or stockbrokers, politicians or professional athletes. Nor, to be honest, do we see it in the mirror as often as we should. When a leader models servanthood, however, group members often follow suit. Being served by others means that we, too, are needy, something our pride denies. That's why the apostle Peter first refused to let Christ wash his feet. Paul describes humility as something we "put on" like a garment. Eugene Peterson in *The Message* translates it as: "Now you're dressed in a new wardrobe. Every item of your new way of life is custom-made by the Creator, with his label on it. All the old fashions are now obsolete.... So, chosen by God for this new life of love, dress in the wardrobe God picked out for you: compassion, kindness, humility, quiet strength, discipline" (Colossians 3:12).

One great way for your group to practice serving is to help people who cannot return the favor or even thank you. Scripture identifies them as the poor, orphan, widow, and stranger. The first letter of each group forms an acrostic: P.O.W.S. In effect, these are prisoners of war—held captive by life's tragedies and trials. Giving to them is nothing like our Christmas giving, when we often receive as well as give presents. But Christlike giving, as you know, includes discovering needs, then serving and loving someone who may be unable to give back. This kind of giving creates an atmosphere of humility in a small group.

A couples group in our church learned of a woman (outside their group) whose husband had just left her with three kids, a big house, and no income. Members decided to mow the lawn and clean the house for an entire summer. To this day only one person in the group has actually met the woman. The others served her in silence, as it were, never meeting her. That's just the way it worked out.

Too often we serve because we long to hear, "Thank you for serving," or we hope for a return favor. But James tells us that true religion is true service—to the poor, orphan, widow, and stranger—to people who can never pay you back (James 1:27). Such service will strip your group of pride.

Authentic relationships develop when people move toward knowing, loving, and serving. This progression fosters intimacy, true caring, and servanthood, so that groups change lives, as God intends. This environment of knowing and being known, of loving and being loved, and of serving and being served paves the way for the challenging yet rewarding work of truth-telling.

## Truth-Telling: To Admonish and Be Admonished

So far, building authentic small group relationships has sounded great. But admonish and be admonished? Most of us would rather have a root canal than enter the potential relational chaos when one sister admonishes another in community. Yet, since our church began in 1975, Willow Creek has worked on speaking and hearing the truth. We value admonishing almost as much as we value the Willow mantras "lost people matter to God" and "turning irreligious people into fully devoted followers of Christ."

It takes work by our leadership core and effort in small groups—of sometimes Herculean magnitude—to put the value into practice. We persist because the Scriptures command us. Truth-telling creates problems when neglected, but it creates spiritual growth when done right. Consider these biblical imperatives (our emphasis):

- "We proclaim him, *admonishing* and teaching everyone with all wisdom, so *that we may present everyone perfect* in Christ. To this end I labor, struggling with all his energy, which so powerfully works in me" (Colossians 1:28–9).
- "Let the *peace* of Christ rule in your hearts, since as members of one body *you were called to peace*. And be thankful. Let the word of Christ dwell in you richly as you teach and *admonish* one another with all wisdom, and *as you sing psalms, hymns and spiritual songs* with gratitude in your hearts to God" (Colossians 3:15–16).
- "Dear brothers and sisters, honor those who are your leaders in the Lord's work. They work hard among you and *warn you* against all that is wrong. Think highly of them and give them your *wholehearted love* because of their work. And remember to *live peaceably* with each other" (1 Thessalonians 5:12–13 NLT).

"Admonish" comes from the Greek *noutheteo,* meaning "to put in mind" or "to warn," and is thus a form of teaching. Though primarily corrective, admonition, as in the above verses, is often linked with teaching, encouraging, and edification. The ministry of admonishing calls people to change, then provides encouragement and teaching to help them change. It is an expression of genuine love and truth from which there can be no turning.

Yet, fearing conflict, we often avoid truth-telling. What message have you often spoken in your mind but never said aloud to a loved one? Write out the exhortation or affirmation you wish you could say. Now, what's holding you back from telling? Most likely you worry you'll hurt, anger, or embarrass the other person (or yourself). Perhaps you wonder whether you have the right to speak tough words, whether it's more Christlike to avoid conflict and disagreement. Henry Cloud, a Christian psychologist, has counseled thousands of people whose families subtly but consistently

enforced nonengagement. He lists these unspoken rules in his book
*Changes That Heal*:

> Thou shalt not let anyone get emotionally close to you. Keep your
> distance.
>
> Thou shalt not tell the truth about how you are feeling. If you are
> hurt, keep it a secret.
>
> Thou shalt always lie, if it will keep the peace.
>
> Thou shalt not talk about any family matter outside the home, or
> any hurt that you sustain here. Breaking loyalty is an abomina-
> tion.
>
> Tender feelings are an abomination.[7]

But withholding truth robs people of opportunities for spiritual growth.
Truth is the foundation of any authentic relationship. Truly trusting each
other means speaking and hearing the truth together.

Imagine the following scenario: Ted, a small group leader, and Mark,
a coach who shepherds up to five small group leaders, have been meeting
almost weekly for five years. They hold each other accountable as leaders, fathers, husbands, and believers. Early in their relationship, Ted asked,
"Mark, can I tell you something?" Mark agreed. Ted continued, "When
we talk, you often look past me at everything that's going on behind me.
That communicates that what I say doesn't matter to you. It really both-
ers me."

Sheepishly, Mark joked, "Uh, anything else you want to talk about?"

Ted was tender but direct: "Mark, our relationship matters to you
and me. If we can't help each other and hold each other in check, we're
just going through the motions."

Mark might have shouted back, "Well, excuse me, Mr. Perfect! I've
got an earful for you!" He was tempted—but he cared more about personal growth and friendship. True, he didn't like Ted much for the next
three hours. But he listened to the Holy Spirit's whisper: "It's true. Ted's
right!" That turning point challenged both men to speak and hear truth
in love, respect, and grace. I know, because "Ted" is me (Bill), and
"Mark" is my friend Jim. This really did happen—and we are changed
people.

We have a relationship rooted in trust, love, and hope for genuine
spiritual transformation. Our friendship isn't perfect, but it's authentic.
We seek to live what Ephesians 4:25 commands: "Therefore each of you

must put off falsehood and speak truthfully to his neighbor, for we are all members of one body."

Without admonishing one another, our group life becomes shrouded in pretense, shaped by false assumptions, filled with unmet expectations. Emotions retreat underground, pain is medicated but never relieved, and the relationship we long for becomes just another name on a long list of acquaintances.

When within our groups we know, we love, we serve, and we admonish, then we feel the warmth of Christian community spreading throughout the church. Groups permeate every area of ministry, touching lives in profound ways, just as the first believers did, "praising God and enjoying the favor of all the people" (Acts 2:47). Now let's add the fuel of celebration to the growing fire of authentic relationships! But be warned—such flames are not easily extinguished.

## Affirmation: To Celebrate and Be Celebrated

I (Bill) came to faith and joined a church that seemed to believe that the grumpier you were, the more holy you were. Anyone who smiled a lot was having too much fun, and that meant sin in the camp! When I left my job as a commercial lending officer and went to seminary, my church graciously let me try out what I was learning in school. They let me speak about once every three weeks. I was on the B team, the Sunday night service team. (Everyone knows the A team plays on Sunday morning. On Sunday night, when attendance, interest, and energy are low, you bring out the B team.)

Our unspoken policy stated that anybody who wanted to "bless" the audience with their talents could try on Sunday nights. Testimonies circled but never landed. Mary would say, "God gave me a song," while the rest of us wondered whether God really meant for the rest of us to hear it. I, too, was allowed to inflict my speaking on people, hoping they'd grow and I'd improve.

We B team members did our best but knew we bumbled. We felt vulnerable. We welcomed every affirmation, from "Thanks for bringing the Word to us" and "Good to hear you preach again" to a well-meaning "You'll do better next time" or "Nice tie!" Encouragement gave me hope that maybe, just maybe, I could someday become a teacher or pastor. One woman, though, always waited at the end of the (short) line to share her thoughts. She'd look up at me with somber, irrepressibly sullen eyes and say, "Remember, Bill. We are all just a piece of dirt." Kind of brings a tear to your eye, huh? After all, too much affirmation might give me a big head.

But the Bible doesn't equate gloominess with holiness. Just as Jesus and Paul did, small groups celebrate God's work in our lives. We become reminders to one another that God is gracious, redemption is real, and Christ is at work in us. Celebration is woven throughout the Bible. For example, the angels rejoice over every sinner who repents (Luke 15:10), and you and I are invited to the great hallelujah wedding supper of the Lamb (Revelation 19:9).

Jesus was a master of celebration. Whether turning water into wine at a wedding, exulting with followers who were discovering the kingdom of God firsthand (Luke 10:21–24), or having a meal with a recently redeemed tax collector, Jesus' life was marked by deep joy. He had a contagious love for real people in real life. Joy-robbing Pharisees, full of pretension and self-righteousness, made Jesus angry. But his joy overflowed when he was with small groups of real people doing life and ministry, seeking his kingdom with open hearts.

Even in the Upper Room Jesus spoke of joy. "I tell you this so that my joy may be in you and that your joy may be complete" (John 15:11). When it was nearly time for his arrest, Jesus encouraged his fragile followers: "Your grief will turn to joy. . . . Now is your time of grief, but I will see you again and you will rejoice, and no one will take away your joy. . . . Ask and you will receive, and your joy will be complete" (John 16:20–24).

Paul, who knew suffering, also was acquainted with joy. He understood that groups were intended to spend time in celebration. "Rejoice with those who rejoice" he commanded the Romans (12:15). The believers in Colosse were to teach and admonish one another (Colossians 3:16) but not without also "sing[ing] psalms, hymns and spiritual songs with gratitude in your hearts to God." And (probably) from a prison in Rome, Paul exhorted the Philippians to "Rejoice in the Lord always. I will say it again: Rejoice!" (Philippians 4:4). Indeed he wanted the joy of Christ to "overflow on account of me" (1:26). It was essential for early church groups—and remains so for every group—to pause and celebrate the work of God among us.

We have seen groups really take hold of the practice of celebration. Some put members in the center and speak words of affirmation. Others pause virtually every meeting to honor what God is doing in a life in the group. Groups take photos, paint pictures, write affirming letters, give gifts, and sing praises to make sure that ministry and life are celebrated.

Remember, we live in an affirmation-deprived culture. Just recall the last time you went to work and the boss said, "Karen! You're back! We missed you all weekend. Your contribution, caring attitude, promptness, and work efforts are superb! Wow, I cannot imagine this place without you. I sat there watching the Bears game but all I could think about was how your presence brings light to the rest of the staff. You bring out the best in all of us! It sure will be a dark day around here when you leave! You are virtually irreplaceable!" Happens every Monday, right? Wrong. So make it a practice in groups to give people the encouragement they need.

> And let us consider how we may spur one another on toward love and good deeds. Let us not give up meeting together, as some are in the habit of doing, but let us encourage one another—and all the more as you see the Day approaching. (Hebrews 10:24–25)

## Turning Our Souls toward One Another

If you seek to build a church of small groups, make an unwavering commitment to instill authentic relationships into every group in the church. Weave these five practices—self-disclosure, care giving, humility, truth-telling, and affirmation—into the very fabric of community life. To yield here will compromise your ability to create a thriving network of little communities that have virtually unlimited redemptive potential in your church.

To cultivate a culture of community requires that the quality of group life transcend the traditional experiences of most Bible studies, teams, or committees. It takes intention to move groups from casual acquaintance to a committed fellowship of intimate knowers, extraordinary lovers, humble servants, gracious admonishers, and joyful celebrants. Pursuing such authenticity is risky. *What if I am rejected? What if the church is not ready? How long will it take?*

Yet we cannot afford the luxury of waiting for answers. Each Sunday marks another week of relational deficiency among the redeemed. And it marks another seven days that hungry seekers, who matter deeply to God, will sit outside the gates of that redemptive community, hoping that a few scraps of authentic Christianity will somehow fall from the church's table into their empty hands. The odds are stacked against them.

It's a long shot at best—unless someone leads the way by building a new kind of community, a community where souls face one another. Icenogle says it well:

> Small groups are "faceful" communities. Small groups are only faithful as they receive and reflect a face full of God and one another. Within a faithful small group the leader can bring group members to meet God and each other face to face. Like Moses, the small group leader must have the personal faith and courage to risk the face-to-face vulnerability of encounter even though the rest of the group may turn away in fear. A leader who lets go of the personal protective shield and ventures into the presence of another beckons the whole group to consider likewise.[8]

It is your choice to become such a pastor or small group leader. Now is the time to begin—one life at a time, one leader at a time, one group at a time. Remember, anyone can put together a group. *Bodies in a circle, souls turned away*. Instead, choose to build an authentic relational community. We follow Christ, not convention. We pursue spiritual community, not mere camaraderie.

*Bodies in a circle, souls turned away?* Not here. Not now. Never again.

# Small Groups Are Places Where Truth Meets Life

*Just as the truth, properly believed and used, has power to cre-
ate emotional health within the individual, truth can also heal
relationships. Truth heals what hurts between people as well as
what hurts inside them.*

Dr. William Backus, *Telling Each Other the Truth*

More than most believers, North American Christians are inundated by
biblical wealth. We can read the Bible in over four hundred English trans-
lations, choose among new study Bibles each year, listen to the Bible on
tape, and search it online. The Christian publishing industry is exploding
with Bible-related books, tapes, seminars, and broadcasts. Yet our culture—even the Christian subculture—remains biblically illiterate. As one
truism puts it, "To know and not to do, is not to know."

We have an application crisis, a failure to apply Bible knowledge to
our lives. U.S. President James Monroe said, "The question to be asked
at the end of an educational step is not, 'What has the student learned?'
but 'What has the student become?'" Small groups offer Christians the
rare opportunity of studying the Bible, then holding each other accountable to grow in Christ and the fruits of the Spirit. *If.* This transformation
can happen *if* leaders avoid two common extremes in Bible study and *if*
they learn how to turn questions into discussions and turn common meetings into "holy moments."

## Balancing Life and Truth

Authentic relationships form the foundation of any quality small group.
Once that relational framework is laid we can pour the transforming truth

of God's Word, shoring up the foundation for life change. As we explore this truth within the context of relational integrity, our group will strive for lasting change, reflecting the image and work of Christ in us. Now *that's* a small group.

Experience has taught us that there are two kinds of groups: "truth-focused" groups and "life-focused" groups. Truth-focused groups are content driven and thrive on answers to questions. Life-focused groups are experience driven and thrive on responses to emotions. Neither group produces the kind of transformation to which Christ calls us.

## Truth-Focused Groups

Groups organized primarily for Bible study tend to focus only on studying doctrine and getting "the right answer." Leaders affirm that correct answers, right beliefs, and Bible knowledge mark maturity in this group. Group acceptance depends on one's ability to recognize and agree with a single viewpoint. Those who disagree are often viewed as divisive. Because they discuss truth only at a cognitive level, these groups often mistake right answers as evidence of true spiritual growth.

One of our small group leaders was struggling to build community, so he invited us to attend and give feedback. Let's call him "Mike." After a light dinner, Mike began asking questions from a curriculum. "What did you get for number two, Hank?" After Hank gave his answer, Mike responded, "Good answer! Betty, how about you? What did you understand about number two?"

Betty looked tense. Hank's answer was "good," but her answer was different. She wasn't sure if she was right or wrong. But she wanted to be affirmed, so she said, "I agree with Hank." The discussion droned on till Mike got to Mary, one of those proverbial thorns in a "truth group" leader's side.

True to form, rather than giving answers on the agreed subject, Mary drifted to what was on her mind. Her rambling reply made us think of the old Beatles song "The Long and Winding Road." But in the context of answering Mike, she opened up her soul a bit: "As some of you know, my daughter is still considering marrying an unbeliever she has been dating. We have tried to remind her what God says about this, but she plans on moving ahead regardless. It really makes us sad. Anyway, as I was saying. . . ." Mary then got back to the required answer.

With the intuition of a perceptive leader and the caring heart of a Christlike shepherd, Mike said, "Good answer, Mary. Bob, what did you get for number two?"

Just as someone was about to strike a match to the kindling of community building, Mike doused the flames with a bucket of water. He probably didn't even realize he had done it. But he was guided by the misperception that content is more important than the people for whom it was meant.

## Life-Focused Groups

By contrast, life-focused groups emphasize understanding each other by sharing stories of pain, need, and God's work in their lives. Leaders affirm those who freely express their emotions. The group's guiding value is acceptance—without judgment. Members don't learn to discern and apply scriptural truth to their lives. No one looks another in the eye with grace and truth and says, "God is calling you to change."

During my doctoral program, I (Bill) took a course on group counseling. The professor was brilliant. Every Tuesday, he devoted the first half of our three-hour class to teaching and participation in a model group. He led the twenty of us in a pseudo-group counseling experience, often challenging someone in the circle to lead part of the meeting. During the last half of each class we participated in an encounter group, à la Carl Rogers in the 1970s. The professor divided our class of eighteen women and two men into two groups, with one man in each group. Just me and nine unfamiliar women in a windowless twelve-by-twelve room for ninety minutes of pure joy. Not!

Each day the teaching assistant, also a woman, began the session with, "So, what will we talk about today?" Dead silence—sometimes for ten minutes. In encounter groups, you're supposed to take relational risks, reveal your true self, challenge others in the circle, and stretch your boundaries. This was easy to do in our classroom with our professor, but tough in this "prison cell." No standards, no absolutes, no judging others. Growth was the product of self-disclosure and group feedback. Not one shred of biblical truth in the room, not the remnant of a stray Bible verse—not even a fragment from the Dead Sea Scrolls.

One week a woman brought a doll and talked to the doll, because the doll would not judge her as we would. I couldn't escape, because the teaching assistant guarded the only door. Totally focused on understanding and acceptance, the group was oblivious to the concept of discussing truth principles. I withdrew from the discussion. Suddenly, one graduate student said to me, "I don't like your posture," referring to my lack of participation.

Foolishly, I replied, "OK, I'll change it." I crossed my legs the opposite way and asked, "Is that better?" Every pair of female eyes bored through me faster than a high-speed drill. They ate my lunch for the next twenty minutes, though it seemed like twenty years. I promised God I'd go immediately to an obscure mission field if he would just get me out of that room.

Now, to be truthful, I did learn some things in that group. I was challenged to open up my life, to trust people I knew only briefly, to love non-Christians who disagreed vigorously with me, and to try to listen to people in real pain. Several in the group were headed for divorce or had already experienced such trauma. But that group had no standard of truth, no sure and guiding light on the road to healing and true change. Christian "life-focused" groups can be all too similar. But church-based communities of faith require us to exhort one another, asking, "Doesn't God call us to a higher standard?"

## Transformation-Focused Groups

Your small group may include people who drift toward both extremes. Let's affirm that "truth" groups are right to love sound doctrine and biblical literacy—values increasingly absent even among committed Christians. Let's applaud "life" groups for pursuing self-disclosure, expressing emotions, and recognizing real needs. Our challenge as small group leaders, however, is to guard against entropy. We must continue to move members to that tension point in the middle, where truth and life meet face to face—that place called transformation.

In contrast to groups guided only by doctrine or focused only on personal issues, transformation-focused groups connect truth with life, and life with truth. Groups seeking to change lives explore the truth about God and me—not just me and not just God. Members are not obsessed with information but strive toward transformation. People ask, "How do I become like Jesus Christ?" We reward members for being honest with God and others. Community is built on the foundation of authenticity, not simply acceptance or agreement. Granted, a "come-as-you-are" acceptance is valid. But transformation-focused group members never allow each other to pursue life unchanged.

The goal is what John Ortberg describes as "a well-ordered heart," a heart that is organized around what Jesus would think, say, and do in our place. We venture boldly beyond the realm of a well-informed student or a well-understood self to develop a well-ordered heart, a heart being transformed into Christ's image.

How does one know if you have a truth-focused, life-focused, or transformation-focused group? What do the small groups in your church look like? The chart provides a helpful comparison and opportunity for you to assess your situation.

| Truth-Focused Groups | Life-Focused Groups | Transformation-Focused Groups |
|---|---|---|
| Know the answers to the questions | Know the answers to personal problems | Know the truth about God and me |
| Focus on information—What does it mean? | Focus on introspection—How do I feel? | Focus on transformation—How am I becoming like Christ? |
| Reward members for being right | Reward members for being real | Reward members for being honest with God and others |
| Community is built on principle of agreement | Community built on principle of acceptance | Community is built on principle of authenticity |
| The goal is a well-informed student | The goal is a well-understood self | The goal is a well-ordered heart |

You're probably wondering, "But how do we build transformation-focused groups?" That's our question as well because we each lead a small group. We have discovered that creating transformation-focused groups where truth meets life depends on two key leadership skills: how questions are asked and how meetings are designed.

## Turning Questions into Discussions

Years of formal education have led us to believe that the purpose of asking a question is to get an answer. If, however, we want a group where truth meets life, then we must design questions that help people recognize and apply truth and that build understanding and community. Whether you are creating your own questions from a biblical text or using a specified curriculum, you will have to move from asking questions toward creating discussions.

A curriculum can be either a great help or a barrier, depending on how it is written or used. Remember that curriculum is a servant to the group, not the master. Choose study guides that help groups accomplish their purpose. Consider the spiritual maturity of members, the amount of material devoted to each subject, and the length of time you have each meeting for study. Then choose questions wisely or redesign them to lead people into transformational discussions.

## Make It Focused, Make It Personal

Jesus never said, "All power in heaven and earth has been given to me. Go therefore into all the world and complete the curriculum." You can help your group members recognize and apply biblical truth if you focus your group time and make your questions personal.

Though publishers typically provide ten to twenty questions in a small group study, you don't have to ask each question. Do the math. If everyone in your group of eight answers all ten questions, even if everyone limits each response to a minute, the study will take eighty minutes.

Publishers offer so many questions because they're appealing to people at all levels of growth and ability. New groups need more questions until relationships deepen. Some groups require several questions as icebreakers. Most group leaders aren't trained to develop their own questions. An individual using the study for personal use will be able to work through more questions than a group can.

But you want to focus your group time. So, from all the questions publishers offer, choose (or rephrase) just a handful of questions. You will need one or two brief warm-up questions, then two or three questions designed to evoke deep discussion and interaction.

Good questions are personal. Some queries—"Why do most people lack faith? What two things does this Scripture teach us about faith?"—will provoke worthwhile content-centered discussion. To promote individual or group change, though, you need to move on to personal questions, such as: "We all want to trust God, to believe he is at work in our lives. But we can't always see or feel him at work. Where is your faith most fragile today? What step of faith is God asking you (us) to take and how can we begin that step, even if we are afraid?"

## Make It Interactive, Make It Creative

Asking interactive questions and using creativity will help your group members understand each other and build bonds. Capitalize on small group dynamics by designing interactive questions that prompt people to relate to one another as they answer them. You can do this by sub-grouping, setting up a debate, asking people to take various perspectives on an issue, or working in pairs before presenting ideas and thoughts to the group.

For example, you might say, "As we discuss the vine and branches teaching of John 15, let's divide the group in half. Group A should create a list of attributes and actions of someone connected to Christ. What would such a person be like? Group B should describe the characteristics of a disconnected person—someone not hooked into the vine (Christ). In ten minutes we will compare what we discussed and then determine how each of us can work toward a more connected life."

When leaders ask all the questions, they become the center of attention. Interactive questions help members speak to each other and build relationships rather than direct all their comments to the leader. And with a little work, you can make your interactive questions creative as well. Try using newspaper articles, magazine photos, role playing, even costumes to create questions that provoke memorable discussions.

Here's how one of our family groups created an interactive discussion during the Christmas season.[1] Each family unit was assigned to research part of the Christmas story, explain characters' roles and backgrounds (e.g., Mary, wise men, prophets, angels, Herod), then make a presentation of five to seven minutes. They were free to make it exciting with costumes, music, artwork, whatever.

Some dressed up as shepherds, while others designed a prophecy game based on predictions of Jesus' birth. One boy played a violin as his gift to Jesus, and a pianist played a simplified version of "The Hallelujah Chorus." One family acted out the Magi's visit. A Lebanese member showed her Middle East artifacts and photos of Bethlehem. The discussion was lively, engaging, and spiritually enriching.

That Christmas season meeting was a small group leader's dream. Members talked about it long after the "meeting" had ended. Though no one expects such creative questions and memorable meetings each time, the above example includes ideas you can use. That meeting was based on focused content (Christmas story), personal application, interactive style, creative design—and it fit different learning styles.

## Make It Fit

Some leaders feel most comfortable simply teaching and asking questions. But you probably know that auditory learners like storytelling;

visual learners respond to pictures, videos, and drama; kinesthetic learners do best with hands-on activities. Over the course of many meetings, good leaders appeal to all learning styles so that everyone engages with truth and is nudged toward spiritual growth.

I (Bill) remember one occasion in which my wife asked us to write attributes of God on stones she had brought to the meeting. People chose an attribute that had meant something to them that week and explained why they were grateful for this divine trait. We piled our stones into an Old Testament-style altar. Then we paired up and prayed for each other using those attributes, giving worship to God, and seeking his intervention in our lives.

This meeting was interactive and creative, but I remember it especially because it fit my learning style. I could touch it. I could see it. If you're thinking, "But I'm not the touchy-feely type," then ask others for help. You'll probably find people who would love to try out ideas that fit different learning styles.

Asking artful questions will invite transformational discussions. Without such questions, groups often linger at the water of life change but never drink. Questions must create discussion. But meetings must also lead to moments. Let's look at how Jesus leveraged meetings for transformation, then we'll show how you can follow his example.

## Turning Meetings into Moments

Think of it as one of the greatest small group meetings ever, a window into the life of Jesus' little community. There were no straight-backed chairs—the Twelve reclined at a low table. The Passover meal was underway, and Jews had come to Jerusalem to remember. *Bondage ... blood ... freedom.* Much of their theology was built around remembering. Jesus was about to make this a night they would never forget.

You can be certain that the disciples would have never described Jesus' group as *bodies in a circle ... souls turned away.* His group had had many meetings, and Jesus was a master at making every meeting count. From a miraculous recovery on the stormy Sea of Galilee to a house meeting in Capernaum where Jesus taught them who really was the greatest among them, the disciples had seen it all—until here in the Upper Room. Jesus knew that the Passover pattern would soon be relived. *Bondage ... blood ... freedom.* Only this time he would be the Lamb.

The mood was somber, the stakes high. These were the final moments before (literally) all hell would break loose.

Nevertheless, these "distractions" never drew Jesus off course with his group. Rather, the coming events gave him increasing resolve to treasure this moment in community and to leverage it for teaching, loving, serving, and praying. It would be the most profound group experience they would have prior to the Resurrection. It would mark them forever.

## Jesus and His Group: Creating, Seizing, and Marking Moments

Jesus led his group into spiritual community by creating moments, seizing moments, and marking moments. A moment is the place where the active and obvious presence or power of God is at work in the life of an individual or group.[2]

*Creating moments* means designing an experience that leads your group to a decision or response to God. We invite the Holy Spirit to work in us based on the way we speak, the things we study, the way we act, and the atmosphere we create.

In the Upper Room, Jesus used common activities and elements to create a holy moment. First, he invited his group to the table. Tables are rarely noticed, yet what takes place there can alter history. Marriage proposals, family celebrations, peace negotiations, spiritual friendship, and loving confrontation seek the table as the place of common ground. Second, Jesus picked up an ordinary towel and washed his friends' feet. This common activity, normally performed by slaves, symbolized the love that, ultimately, would lead him to the cross. As the apostle John put it, "Having loved his own who were in the world, he now showed them the full extent of his love" (John 13:1).

To create this moment in the Upper Room, Jesus did more than invite his disciples to the table and pick up the towel of servanthood. He also told them the truth: "I tell you the truth, no servant is greater than his master, nor is a messenger greater than the one who sent him. Now that you know these things, you will be blessed if you do them" (John 13:16–17). By ambushing the group with service, he showed them a side of God they hadn't seen. He helped them understand humility.

Jesus also knew how to *seize moments*—a poor woman placing her last two coins in the offering, dinner at a Pharisee's house, a Samaritan woman at a well—as divinely ordained opportunities for grace, truth, and transformation. In the Upper Room, he seized on an opportunity to confront his group's fear. He said, "My children, I will be with you only a little longer. You will look for me, and just as I told the Jews, so I tell you now: Where I am going, you cannot come. A new command I give you: Love one another. As I have loved you, so you must love one another" (John 13:33–34). He drove the point home by telling them that the entire world would be able to identify them as his followers when they expressed such radical love to one another.

Peter was too preoccupied with Jesus' leaving to think about love. He asked, "Lord, where are you going?" Jesus might have replied, "Hey, didn't you hear what I just said? The new commandment? The radical love?" But he didn't. Instead, he took the opportunity to allay fear and bring hope, to remind his group that he would see them again. It was a tender moment, a holy moment. "Don't let your hearts be troubled, you believe in God, believe also in me."

Jesus also led his group into spiritual community by *marking moments*. His disciples had eaten bread and swallowed wine thousands of times before. But in the Upper Room, Jesus said, "Do this in remembrance of me." Forever after, every time they celebrated that supper, each morsel of bread and sip of wine would take them back to that marked moment. They would remember his words, his embrace, his washing their feet, his promise of the Holy Spirit, his exhortation to stay connected to him like a branch to the vine.

Jesus was so good at marking moments because, unlike many group leaders, he never got so caught up in his agenda that he missed what his group was thinking and feeling. Remember when Jesus asked the disciples what people were saying about his identity? Who did they think he really was? Simon Peter responded by affirming, "You are the Christ, the Son of the living God." Jesus didn't simply say, "Great answer, Simon!" Rather, he recognized the Holy Spirit's work in Peter and marked the moment for the entire group. He answered Peter's affirmation with this visionary proclamation: "You are Peter, and on this rock I will build my church, and the gates of Hades will not prevail against it" (Matthew 16:18 NRSV).

Jesus created, seized, and marked these moments because he wanted to do more than have meetings. He wanted to see people change, to see lives transformed by truth.

## You and Your Group: Common Activities or Holy Moments?

Jesus never inadvertently ushered the Spirit out the door instead of inviting him to stay and dine. But do you wonder whether you can move beyond "meetings as usual"? Jesus promises that with him, all things are possible—holy moments, spiritual transformation, true community. Whether focused on a task, Bible study, or prayer, most group meetings have five common components. Here's how you can redesign these components into holy moments.

### Icebreakers: Self-Description or Self-Disclosure?

Such classic meeting starters as "Let's all go around and share our favorite color!" are about as exciting as watching paint dry. Icebreakers fail when used mostly for self-description. But icebreakers designed for self-disclosure will build community.

Here's an icebreaker that has resulted in holy moments at Willow Creek. We ask people to choose a partner, pretend they are fabulously rich, then answer this question: "Using these four categories—luxury, high performance, off-road, vacation/travel—choose an automobile and describe why you'd buy it." We're especially interested in *why* people choose a vehicle.

Leaders gather partners back into groups, then lower group defenses with a little fun. "How many of you picked a luxury vehicle? If you did, welcome to the ranks of the greedy. Just kidding. How many wanted a high performance car? Take a look. These are the people in mid-life crisis. Just ask them how old they are. It tips you right off. Now who wanted an off-road vehicle? These are your typical rule-breakers. You say to these people, 'Pick A, B, or C,' and these people always choose 'D.' Now, finally, who picked the motor coach, the family travel van? See, these people don't get out enough."

Then the leader goes deeper. "Bob, you chose a high performance vehicle because you like adventure. I wonder what the Christian life would look like if we lived it in high performance mode? Janet, you said you are the 'off-road,' risk-taking type. I wonder what it would look like in the eyes of God for you to take a spiritual risk?"

Already the group has moved from the hypothetical purchase of an SUV to an introspective look at spiritual issues and decisions. We can take someone from self-description ("I'd buy a four wheeler") to self-disclosure ("My Christian life would really have to change if I were to take a risk with God"). This kind of icebreaker centers our conversation on choices, on what God is asking us to do by faith as parents, coworkers, or church members. It turns a common activity into a holy moment.

### Bible Study: "So-So" or So What?

Study is another common group activity, even in task groups with limited time. Most groups use a curriculum to help them study Scripture. It's up to the leader to move the group from debating content to applying truth to members' lives.

Consider this question from a curriculum for Hebrews 12:1. The verse concerns "running the race set before us" and exhorts us to "throw off everything that hinders" so we can run for the prize. The curriculum poses the question, "What are some problems some Christians have running the race?" If we stop here, we will never get to the heart of the issue.

I (Bill) lead a small group early every Wednesday morning. One man always pushes us toward application: "So, what are we going to do about this?" Members answer, and he asks, "Well, then why not now?" Someone replies, "Frankly, because I don't feel like it." Now that's like throwing down the gauntlet in a men's group. You can get great content in a book or sermon or on tape. But the small group is the only place where someone will look you in the eye and say, "So what?" Don't be satisfied with merely sharing common information when you can use Bible study for transformation, creating a moment where truth meets life.

### Group Sharing: My Story or God's Story?

How do you move from self-disclosure—the common activity of sharing your story—to God's story? Within nine months, one of the guys in my small group experienced an incredible streak of trouble. Dave's father-in-law was injured falling off a ladder; Dave's two-year-old son had surgery; his close friend's wife died of a brain tumor; two family friends suffered miscarriages (one in the eighth month); his company closed his department. And then Dave had an emergency appendectomy—the same weekend his father had a stroke.

Our group rallied around his needs and prayed fervently for him. That alone was enough to fulfill standard operating procedures for healthy small group functioning. But because we cared about Dave's growth as well as his pain, one man created a moment and asked, "So, what is the Holy Spirit teaching you during this difficult time when it looks like your world is falling apart? What is your relationship with God like now?" Our group quickly moved to a holy place because we knew that Dave's relationship with God was the most significant event in the meeting.

We were not content to leave him in his story. He had to connect with God's story. It is incumbent upon the leader to create this kind of sharing. Don't simply leave them in their story. Connect them with God's story, as Henri Nouwen described: "It is the grateful recognition of God's call to share life together and the joyful offering of a hospitable space where the recreating power of God's Spirit can become manifest. Thus all forms of life together can become ways to reveal to each other the real presence of God in our midst."[3]

Never hesitate to boldly provoke your group to see God's holy presence amid life's triumphs or trials.

## Prayer: Talking to God or Listening to God?

Ever been in a small group at prayer time? Groups always do the circle prayer. It comes toward you like a great white shark to a hapless swimmer. Reminds you of a *Jaws* remake. (Dun-da-dun-da-dun-da.) Praying aloud is especially intimidating for beginners. Three prayers before your turn, sweat beads your forehead. (Dun-da-dun-da-dun-da.) Mary prays, "Oh, most omnipotent and judicious Creator of the cosmos, Father of the Light of lights, Jesus Christ, very God of very God, begotten not made, being of one substance with the Father, great propitiator of sin . . ." Neither Billy Graham nor Mother Theresa could compete with that.

Oblivious to the next prayer, you decide simply to thank God for his protection this week. Even though you consider getting a master's degree in theology before the next meeting, you are ready. Then something almost as evil as the curse takes place. Mike, sitting to your left, prays, "Thank you, God, for your protection this week." You are stunned and angry. "He prayed my prayer! God, that's not fair!" In a nervous moment you thank God for air and hope no one recognized your voice.

Prayer is one of the most awe-inspiring yet frustrating components of any small group. Groups should be the place where we explore the creativity and wonder of prayer together. Through time and intention, prayer can produce a robust appreciation for God's work in us. Episcopalian spiritual director Margaret Guenther enlightens us on prayer:

> To listen for God is to be engaged in a counter-cultural enterprise, for much in our daily lives works against the patient labor of attentiveness.

Our world is noisy, seemingly addicted to sound and distraction. Our world is busy; wasting time is one of our national sins. Yet attending to the holy is slow work, a work of gradual growth and fruition rather than measurable production or conquest.[4]

Prayers of blessing, confession, hope, and intercession should mark small groups. Let us pray in pairs, pray silently, write prayers in journals. Let us pray for lost friends and broken families, character growth and physical healing, biblical wisdom and ordinary, everyday courage. Let the conversation of prayer flow from our lips easily, like words to a friend or a lover. And let us move to listening to God as much as we do talking to him. But for goodness sakes, let's break the circle.

## Group Tasks: Satisfy Self or Serve Others?

One final way of turning meetings into moments is serving together. Many Willow Creek groups are organized for the purpose of serving others. Other groups soon discover service as an essential component of group life. To ensure that truth meets life in service, leaders must call groups to evaluate their motivation for serving. Do we want to do a good deed and check it off our list, or do we want to invite God to change us as we serve others?

Once, while working with task group leaders, I (Bill) asked people to jot down their understanding of their group's mission or purpose. I asked two ushers to share the purpose of their task. The first man said, "Our job is to make sure everybody who comes in here finds a seat quickly." He honorably stated the group's basic requirements.

The next usher, however, took a different approach. "I think our mission is to ensure that people have an undistracted experience from the time they walk in the building to the time they get to their seats, so they can hear the Spirit of God at work through the message and through the music. And it's my job to pay attention to what's happening in their lives, so that I might speak a word of truth or encouragement to them, if the need arises." That guy gets it! He understands the difference. And you could see the mood around that table change. This was a fun exercise until that guy talked. The other ushers looked at their cards and conspicuously slid them under the table. Now they understood the difference between a meeting and a moment, between a cause and an activity—and they knew they could do better.

It is easy to miss the heart of the moment when we focus simply on completing a task. Another pitfall is seeing service as a means of self-promotion. You pick up a person who needs gas for their car. After you help them to a station, a little voice inside says, "Great job! You were incredible! Others just drove right past the guy. But you stopped and picked him up. Yep, they just don't make 'em like you anymore!" When you hear that voice, you remember your sinful nature. But when you serve others and seek God to do a work in you, he will redeem you from that voice.

## A Race to the Finish

We've got to decide, friends, whether we will be a people who have common meetings or holy moments. You and I are in a race to connect people to lifesaving community. It begins and ends with intention. We must lead people into encounters with God's Spirit and Word. Instead of asking questions to get answers, we must begin to turn questions into discussions—discussions that bring the community face to face with truth and life. We must help one another create, seize, and mark moments that invite the presence, power, and activity of the risen Christ into our lives.

We must run persistently against all that destroys community—divisiveness, fear, pride, and self-interest. We have a chance to build a community where truth meets life and produces transformation. But we race against time. How long can we allow groups merely to have meetings instead of experiencing moments? How long must we wait before challenging one another to spiritual growth? Do we have the courage to start the race—and then run it all the way to the end?

The Olympic Games in Mexico City, 1968, were filled with the usual incredible performances. Swimmer Mark Spitz captured seven gold medals, and world records fell like autumn leaves on a windy October day. But as is often the case, one human drama exemplified the true meaning of sport, often lost in today's feeding frenzy for endorsements and movie contracts.

Out of the cold darkness he came. John Stephen Akwari of Tanzania entered at the far end of the stadium, pain hobbling every step, his leg bloody and bandaged. The winner of the Olympic marathon had been declared over an hour earlier. Only a few spectators remained, but the lone runner pressed on. As he crossed the finish line, the small crowd roared out its appreciation, "Yea!" Afterward, a reporter asked the runner why he had not retired from the race, since he had no chance of winning. He seemed confused by the question. Finally he answered, "My country did not send me to Mexico City to start the race. They sent me to finish."

Do you want to put on the uniform and go through warm-ups? Or do you want to finish the race? Building a church of groups is like running a marathon. It is a long trek in the same direction. It begins with God's design for community and then leads to an understanding of what makes a group into a community. At the core is a clear commitment to build authentic relationships and then to design groups as places where truth meets life. As people begin to deepen relationships, two more areas need to be addressed—experiencing healthy conflict and shepherding people toward full devotion to Christ. Community demands it. The Bride of Christ is worth it. And we must settle for nothing less.

# Small Groups Experience Healthy Conflict

*When my thrust as a person—my hopes, dreams, wants, needs, drives—runs counter to your thrust, there is conflict. To sacrifice my thrust is to be untrue to the push and pull of God within me. To negate your thrust is to refuse to be reverent before the presence and work of God within you. Caring, confronting, and integrating your needs and wants with my needs and wants in our joint effort toward creating Christian community is what effective living is all about.*

DAVID AUGSBURGER, *CARING ENOUGH TO CONFRONT*

For three years I (Russ) had a challenging relational dynamic with one of my small group members. That's a euphemistic way of saying we didn't get along. Our chronic conflict was particularly troublesome because we were both church leaders and because our small group promised that we would all tell each other "the last ten percent." Telling the last ten percent is Bill Hybels' great way of explaining what it means to speak the truth in love—including the parts you are afraid to say.

I will never forget the defining conversation we had when, with great care and forthrightness, we finally spoke the last ten percent to each other. We were running together one day, between group meetings, to build our relationship. As one of us tiptoed into the sensitive territory of our conflicts, the other responded with openness. That got us talking about each other's "spiritual growth edges" (read "character defects"). Next we acknowledged how many of our conflicts were rooted in old-fashioned sin: we confronted each other about perceived patterns of envy and pride. We spoke the last ten percent on several topics.

In one forty-five-minute run, deep conversation presented stark mirrors of truth. But it also led to new and resolved community. Since then, neither of us can believe how our relationship has grown. Meanwhile, the mirroring we did for each other has produced exciting growth in both of us. We can't imagine now not being in community together and not having the maturity gained by how we ministered to each other. What had sometimes been destructive conflict has been resolved; that which could have ruined community and ministry has brought relational health. But we had to embrace conflict as a part of small group life.

When groups avoid conflict, they turn their backs on true community. One cannot exist without the other. David Augsburger explains, "I can come to see conflict as *natural, neutral, normal*. I may then be able to see the difficulties we experience as tensions in relationships and honest differences in perspective that can be worked through by caring about each other and each confronting the other with truth expressed by love."[1]

*Truth expressed by love.* Can you hear the echoes of Ephesians 4? Paul gave us this dictum because he wanted all the churches to get it right. He understood healthy conflict as a fundamental building block for Christian community.

- "Instead, speaking the truth in love, we will in all things grow up into him who is the Head, that is, Christ." (Ephesians 4:15)
- "So put away all falsehood and 'tell your neighbor the truth' because we belong to each other." (Ephesians 4:25 NLT)
- "Do not let any unwholesome talk come out of your mouths, but only what is helpful for building others up according to their needs, that it may benefit those who listen." (Ephesians 4:29)

When truth meets life in the context of authentic relationships, conflict is inevitable. Community demands that members face tensions and disagreements with direct, loving communication—rather than letting resentment, hidden emotions, and unresolved anger unravel the community. Truth, spoken in love, means that we want the best for others. Healthy conflict can be a tool the Holy Spirit uses to shape us into Christ's image.

The familiar proverb "Iron sharpens iron" reminds us that growth is hard. Rather than work through healthy conflict, however, groups sometimes allow members to drift unaware into relational, moral, or even physical disaster. In my (Bill) men's group, we have learned the blessings of exhorting each other toward necessary behavioral change or correct biblical thinking. One member had discerned it was God's will that he move to California. His wife agreed. Yet he was afraid to follow God's guidance because it meant leaving a steady job, a network of meaningful relationships, and Willow Creek ministries to which he, his wife, and their sons were very committed.

We could have functioned as a "nice" little group. "We're still praying that you will make that decision, Ken. Of course, we will just wait and see what God does. We know it's hard. After all, it may not be God's will for your life. Hang in there and let us know if there is anything we can do." Instead, we confronted and challenged him to replace fear with faith, to trust and obey God's call. The changes that have taken place since he answered that call testify to God's work in and through him.

Whether conflict achieves the Holy Spirit's purpose depends on how leaders handle it. The small group leader who understands how she must, from time to time, encourage healthy conflict resolution will serve her group in ways that will transform it and its members. As the group welcomes periodic conflict as a community-builder, it will move into intimacy unavailable to those who avoid it.

Working through healthy conflict is like going to school. Each learning experience builds on the next. First you learn the elementary principles of dealing with face-to-face conflict. Then you advance to managing conflict within a group. Finally, you will graduate to knowing how to love people into true restoration after conflict.

## Elementary Conflict Resolution: The Biblical Foundation

The Bible gives two reasons for group members to enter the process of conflict resolution, and it explains why leaders must guide their groups through this process. The two reasons for conflict resolution are confronting unrepentant or unconfessed sin and reconciling relational breakdown.

Matthew 18:15–20 is our guide for *confronting sinful behavior in others*: "If another believer sins against you, go privately and point out the fault. If the other person listens and confesses it, you have won that person back. But if you are unsuccessful, take one or two others with you and go back again, so that everything you say may be confirmed by two or three witnesses. If that person still refuses to listen, take your case to the church. If the church decides you are right, but the other person won't accept it, treat that person as a pagan or a corrupt tax collector" (Matthew 18:15–17 NLT).

Around Willow Creek "doing a Matthew 18" is part of our culture and working vocabulary. Whether a person has obviously sinned and not repented or is ignorant of a sinful pattern, we must lovingly but directly confront that person. Following Matthew 18 we begin personally, one-on-one with the offender. If the person doesn't respond, we involve accountable partners, and, if necessary, take the issue to the church leaders. We follow this biblical pattern to preserve the unity and testimony of Christ's body.

We also begin conflict resolution *when relationships break down*. In Matthew 5:23–24 Jesus exhorted his hearers to reconcile relationships with fellow believers before offering worship to God. In effect, our worship is void if we are at odds with brothers and sisters in Christ. Leave your gift. Don't present it to God until you've repaired relationships. On one occasion that Bill Hybels taught this passage, he actually gave people permission to leave the church service to reconcile a relationship. He encouraged us to move throughout the auditorium and speak with anyone we needed to. Some made phone calls; others met briefly in the lobby. Still others sat next to one another, expressing feelings and asking for forgiveness.

Conflict resolution is not simply preached—our leaders pursue it faithfully. The elders at Willow Creek Community Church have insisted that conflict resolution be resolved according to Matthew 18. Besides having seen nearly every kind of relational breakdown here, many serve as mediators outside of Willow Creek. Their wise interventions have protected the Bride of Christ and moved people to biblical reconciliation.

## Advanced Conflict Resolution: Reconciliation in Groups

We place a strong emphasis on conflict resolution because, in building a church of groups, relational discord is more common than unrepented sin. Prideful people bruise each other's egos and offend each other with harsh words and inconsiderate actions. Even though we affirm that conflict can transform relationships, we know how hard it is to work through relational minefields in healthy, God-honoring ways.

In tenth grade, I (Bill) had an experience that illustrates the role small group leaders must sometimes assume during conflict. As a sophomore, I hung around with a few rebels who reveled in annoying the administration. We plugged test tubes in the chemistry lab, stapled dismembered frogs (dissected during anatomy class) to the walls of the English room, and rearranged seats to confuse substitute teachers. Things escalated when we dared John to light a firecracker in the cafeteria. There it sat on a lunch table, in a milk carton, invisible except for its small fuse. We egged John on until he mustered the guts to light the firecracker and push it down the table. It exploded, showering nearby students with pasteurized paste. We erupted in raucous laughter. It was the highlight of the semester.

The supervisor, who was also my chemistry teacher, herded the nine of us to the vice principal's office. The vice principal questioned my friend Howard, the first guy in line. Howard made only one mistake—he told the truth. He said he dared John to do it. The vice principal turned to his assistant and said, "Get Howard's mother on the phone." Howard blanched as his mother's voice crackled at the other end of that ugly black phone. Then, he asked the rest of us, one at a time, to reveal our role in the conspiracy. One at a time, we coughed out words we'd been rehearsing since hearing Howard's mother. "John did it. And I never said a word. Before I knew it there was an explosion!"

It's no fun to be the vice principal—to confront people, say hard words, and seek truth. As Willow Creek small group leaders agreed at a recent retreat, most of us would rather wear the vision caster hat or the shepherd hat or the encourager hat. We cringe at wearing the vice principal hat, because we don't like to confront anyone, even when we know the confrontation is necessary. Yet, the "vice principal hat" is a fitting metaphor for a leader's role in conflict, because, as Paul told Timothy, God calls us to "correct, rebuke and encourage—with great patience and careful instruction" (2 Timothy 4:2).

Whether conflict just happens or has been brewing over time, we need to confront it and move toward reconciliation. Otherwise the destructive words and damaged emotions will jeopardize our group life. Before confronting conflict, however, it's wise to pray and emotionally prepare. As group leader, you must set boundaries for when and how to handle conflict in meetings. Then, within these ground rules, you must follow certain guidelines for navigating the breakdown.

## Prayer and Emotional Preparation

Pray first for discernment. Each person involved must ask, "Is there a real conflict, or am I simply suffering from wounded pride or a bruised ego?" If the Spirit of God confirms that the other person did not do anything wrong, then you can avoid unnecessary conflict. Your task, instead, is to deal with your own reaction and feelings.

I (Bill) watched my wife deal with such a situation. As a women's ministry coach, Gail provided care, development, and support to five small group leaders. During a huddle (our term for leaders' meetings), one leader felt that Gail offended her. Gail told me, "I need to tell this leader I'm sorry."

I asked, "What did you do?" She described how the woman had misunderstood some of Gail's direct but loving remarks to her huddle. I then asked, "Is there anything you did—either in your heart or anywhere else—that was wrong or out of line biblically or relationally with this person?"

Gail thought for a moment and said no.

"Then what are you apologizing for?" I asked.

My question caught her off guard. There was nothing for which to apologize. The other woman had chosen to add an unintended meaning to the interaction. Careful not to declare "case closed," I offered this advice, "Pray through this before you talk with her. My sense, from what you told me, is that you have no obligation except listen to her and acknowledge her feelings." She took it before God, and asked the leader to do the same. When they talked again, they could lovingly work through the leader's feelings and move forward with the relationship. Prayer invited the Holy Spirit to bring conviction and clarity to the interaction and allowed both women to reflect on their hearts, motives, and behavior.

Before confronting conflict, group members must also pray about their words. Pray that God will give you the words and approach to reach the other person. Try writing out your key points, so you won't ramble. Rehearsing aloud may give you insight into how your words will sound to another.

Finally, ask God to give you ears to hear the response and eyes to see the other person's expressions. Once we speak words of truth or conviction, it's time to observe their reception. Are the hearers angry, resentful, confused, shocked? Did they really hear what you said—or only what *they* wanted to hear? Your intentional listening and clarifying may make or break the meeting.

Few of us are trained from birth to be emotionally sensitive to other people's needs and responses. That's why you need to emotionally prepare people for the words you'll say. You need to enter a conflict situation willing both to speak and hear truth.

Russ is good at preparing someone for a difficult discussion. He was my supervisor at the church before I began working for the Willow Creek

Association. He needed to challenge me on some performance issues. But instead of firing away, he prepared me by saying, "Look, Bill, in a few minutes we're going to talk about a range of issues in your department. Some items relate to strategy and personnel decisions. But then I want to discuss an issue that may require difficult words. I have a few observations about our working relationship, and I want to explore some solutions for areas I believe need some work on your part. I am confident we can resolve it together."

Do you see what he did? First, he let me prepare emotionally for an awkward conversation. Rather than catch me off guard, he let me compose myself outwardly, even though inside I was saying, "Ahhhhh! What problems? Okay, calm down. Hard words are coming, so think clearly and respond appropriately. Okay, I'm ready now."

Second, he described a conversation that would address issues and give me a chance to respond. That let me know he wasn't coming to do battle so he could win the war and leave me bleeding.

Third, he told me our relationship mattered to him, that he believed we could work through the problem.

Now, let me be clear. The conversation was still difficult and awkward at times. But because we each had a chance to prepare, it moved along very well. Most important, we both learned a lot about each other, and it was a turning point in our long-term relationship.

If groups thrive on authentic relationships that integrate truth and life, then healthy conflict resolution is essential. After laying the groundwork of prayer and emotional preparation, we must agree to ground rules so we can confront and reconcile with grace and honor.

## Setting Boundaries for Managing Group Conflict

You know you need to pray and prepare for confronting conflict, but perhaps you wonder: What about conflicts that arise in a group meeting? What does a leader do? How does a group handle it? These basic guidelines will help you process group conflict in a group meeting.

### Rule 1: If It Happens in the Group, Process It in the Group

Sandy and Mike disagree over how to parent a wayward teen. Not a big problem, until Sandy says, "If you really cared about Peter, you would take away his car!" This personal attack will probably elicit a defensive and equally toxic response. Group members often debate issues and doctrines. But when someone implies that another member has inferior character or misplaced motives, it gets ugly. When this happens within the group, the group has to deal with it at some level.

### Rule 2: The Leader Is Responsible for Process, Not Outcomes

As leaders we have group agendas. We want to study Scripture, discuss decisions, provide care, plan events, and facilitate meetings. We don't want agenda disruptions. Unresolved conflict definitely upsets the agenda. Leaders may be tempted to quickly reconcile the parties involved, then get on with the program. But the conflict may be the real program, providing an extraordinary teachable moment for spiritual growth within your group.

Instead of focusing on outcomes ("I sure hope Phil and Steven will get along after this"), shine your laser beam on the process by setting discussion guidelines and holding people accountable. Decide how much time you will devote to discussion and remind members to uphold core values. (These values, along with your vision and purpose for the group, are best put in writing as a group covenant.)[2] Counsel members to show respect, speak truth in love, maintain an open heart, and really listen to each other. Exercise your spiritual authority as leader by outlining expectations for follow up and accountability. Discuss what you expect from the people who butted heads, what the group hopes will happen between meetings, and when the involved parties will present a status report.

### Rule 3: Validate the Conflict

Strange as it sounds, you should affirm the group for dealing with conflict. You might say, "I commend you for viewing this group as a safe place to reveal deep feelings. That is wonderful. Few people risk being truthful about God, themselves, and others. Your expressions and thoughts—even your quiet reflections—show you are willing to work on your own soul. Second, your commitment to enter into a process together displays humility. No one is saying that they have it all right and the rest of us are wrong. You are pursuing what God wants—spiritual growth for each person here."

### Rule 4: The Conflict Need Not Be Resolved at This Meeting

People often need time to process emotions, reconnect with God, explore the origin of their feelings, and choose their words. Allow the group to live in the tension of unresolved conflict. It will force them to seek God, to recognize that life is sometimes messy.

### Rule 5: Conflict Must Be Processed with Trust and Confidentiality

After people express strong feelings, they often feel awkward and wish they could retract or restate their words. Their souls are fragile, their spirits weak. Remind—or exhort, if necessary—members to maintain the covenant value of confidentiality. Only then will members be able to resolve the conflict.

## Navigating Breakdown

The following guidelines apply whether you are navigating conflict between members or as an entire group. You may need to put on the vice principal hat and speak some hard truth. Or perhaps it's time for a "heart-to-heart" with a brother or sister who rubs you the wrong way.

### Guideline 1: Start Soon

You may need space to settle your emotions, but don't put off conflict for two weeks. Reconcile as soon as you can. I (Bill) remember an emotional conversation with a staff member in another church. The discussion remained biblical, but started to heat up. My frustrated colleague said, "Well, nine months ago you offended me when you said. . . ." Nine months ago! I wondered what other offenses he had filed away. Frankly, for nine months I felt fine. But he let this offense eat at his soul for nine months rather than bring it up with me.

### Guideline 2: Meet Face to Face

Not e-mail! A Willow Creek leader received a stinging e-mail from a man in his small group. Instead of phoning for an appointment, the leader fired back a zinger. After several electronic exchanges, he realized: "Uh-oh, I shouldn't have done the e-mail thing." This was the understatement of the week. He is a good leader but let his emotions get the best of him. Their online communication created a permanent record of words but robbed them of the chance to read emotions, faces, and tone of voice. Snail mail has the same drawbacks.

### Guideline 3: Affirm the Relationship

Remind people that you are trying to resolve this conflict precisely because you care about them and about your relationship. The way Russ confronted me about performance affirmed that he wanted to build on what we had. Now, years after that confrontation, here we are writing a book together. Because we sought to work it through biblically, we have a deepening friendship and close working relationship.

### Guideline 4: Make Observations, Not Accusations

It's one thing to say, "Now, Bob, I've asked for that report three times and each time you promised that you would give it to me 'the next day.' As I understand the situation, this is a broken promise and a lack of commitment to the work we need to get done. It is unacceptable. I feel that you do not respect my authority, and we need to resolve this immediately." It's another thing to blurt out, "Bob, you're a liar! Three times you told me you would do this and you haven't. You're a liar!" The first approach is firm and direct but involves making observations about what is seen, heard, felt, and understood. The second approach is an accusation. Calling Bob a liar is a character assassination. It puts his character in question and places him on the defensive.

### Guideline 5: Get the Facts

Besides offering your own observations, be sure to let the other person respond. You might say, "Here's what I saw, heard, and felt; now, what did *you* see? What do *you* understand about this situation? Am I missing something?"

### Guideline 6: Promote Resolution

The point of navigating conflict is not to fight, win, or prove who's more holy; it is to restore relationships we value. We want to reach consensus and move forward. Sometimes that may mean agreeing to disagree or deciding to overlook an offense for the sake of the relationship. In either case, we agree not to resurrect the offense. We decide together what next steps, if any, must be taken on the road to resolution—and we abide by them. Trust has been broken. Sticking to the arrangement will rebuild some of that trust.

## Graduate Level Conflict Resolution: True Restoration

Having moved through elementary and advanced levels of conflict resolution, you will still want to help your group finish well and achieve true loving restoration. Many of us, especially men, have trouble saying, "I'm sorry. I was wrong. Forgive me." Yet for conflict resolution to yield spiritual growth within community, group members must engage in the biblical triad of confession, forgiveness, and reconciliation. Once truth has been spoken or a conflict is being processed, those involved must submit. Otherwise conflicts will degenerate to finger pointing and win-lose propositions devoid of grace and truth.

## Confession

In his book *The Life You've Always Wanted* John Ortberg clarifies confession, a misunderstood spiritual discipline: "Confession is not primarily something God has us do because he needs it. God is not clutching tightly to his mercy, as if we have to pry it from his fingers like a child's last cookie. We need to confess in order to heal and be changed. . . . When we practice confession well, two things happen. The first is that we are liberated from guilt. The second is that we will at least be a little less likely to sin in the same way in the future than if we had not confessed. Sin will look and feel less attractive."[3]

We practice confession within our small groups so we may reconcile. We own our sin—pride, envy, rash judgments, love withheld—and acknowledge it to those we've hurt. An authentic confession, one that reflects the heart, lowers defenses and opens hearts to healing.

By contrast, Gordon MacDonald, now of the Trinity Forum and formerly pastor of Grace Chapel in Lexington, Massachusetts, describes a testimony he heard from a young singer. The young man said: "I was sinking deep, deep in sin [which is really a plagiarism of an old Baptist hymn] I was drifting further, further away from God. There was no temptation I did not face, no kind of evil that I wasn't attracted to [sic]. I was rebellious, defiant, and destructive. And then, praise God, *at the age of four*, I came to Jesus, and he changed my life."[4] Such confessions leave us wondering whether the people are sincere. Can a four-year-old experience a deep change of heart?

It's important to keep our small group communications truthful and open, yet respectful of boundaries. The point of confession is neither to impress nor shock group members. Inappropriate confession can damage trust and fracture fragile relationships. The level of confession is directly proportional to the depth of trust and love in a relationship. And it is inversely proportional to the size of a small group. Deeper levels of confession are often found with two or three people than with ten or twelve. So it is important to begin small and simple, until a group creates the safety and accountability to move to greater levels of confession.

Here are guidelines for appropriate confession that will produce personal transformation and group cohesion.

| Guidelines for Confession |
|---|
| 1. *Address* everyone involved (Psalm 32:5; Luke 19:8; James 5:16). |
| 2. *Avoid* using "if," "but," and "maybe." What excuses or blaming do you need to avoid? |
| 3. *Admit* specifically what was done or said (Ezra 9:5–15). |
| 4. *Apologize:* How might others feel as a result of your sin? |
| 5. *Accept* the consequences (Luke 15:19; 19:8). |
| 6. *Alter* your behavior. What changes do you intend to make, with God's help, in the way you think, speak, and behave in the future? (Matthew 3:8; Acts 26:20). |
| 7. *Ask* for forgiveness and allow time. What might make the person whom you have wronged reluctant to forgive you? |

Adapted from Ken Sande, *The Peacemakers Workbook* (Grand Rapids: Baker, 1993).

If you have offended the group, then it is appropriate to confess to the group. For example, the Holy Spirit makes a member realize his pattern of making negative comments and blaming others within the group. Knowing he has acted wrongly, a man confesses his arrogance and toxic communication to the group and asks for forgiveness. This is a holy moment—one the leader may choose to seize or gloss over. This group now holds the keys to life and death, blessing and curse. By receiving the confession, proclaiming forgiveness, and embracing the man with love and respect, this group can make a quantum leap into a new level of community.

James, seeking to encourage and exhort a scattered group of Jewish believers, addresses the healing nature of communal confession: "And their prayer offered in faith will heal the sick, and the Lord will make them well. And anyone who has committed sins will be forgiven. *Confess your sins to each other* and pray for each other so that you may be healed" (James 5:15–16 NLT, emphasis ours).

Notice how James links healing and confession. He knows that sin has spiritual and physical consequences, that physical healing sometimes flows from confession and forgiveness. Confessing to trusted members of our groups will build greater community, establish trust, and remind us that we are all weak, desperately needing one another. Our groups become places that meet self-disclosure with grace, treat broken hearts with tender love, and confront relational discord with truth.

## Forgiveness

Confession unlocks the door of community. Forgiveness invites us in. Henri Nouwen often said that forgiveness is allowing the other person not to be God. To withhold forgiveness is to demand perfection in the life of others. The heart that refuses to forgive is a heart that will never fully heal. Instead it will harden with resentment, bitterness, and rage.

But if true love keeps no record of wrongs (1 Corinthians 13:5), then why forgive? Why not just forget? After all, Proverbs 19:11 says, "People with good sense restrain their anger; they earn esteem by overlooking wrongs" (NLT). If wronged, why not just let it slide? It appears the wisdom from Proverbs here applies to the unintended offense that should be set aside. Later the writer warns against being a hot-tempered person. Thus, in this case, it presupposes that the consequences are nominal and that no grave injustice has been committed. The work required to confront, expose, and correct the offense is disproportionate to the damage caused.

However, when patterns of sin disrupt or threaten the unity of the Spirit, or when groups cannot be reconciled, confession and forgiveness must take place in the community. To forgive someone acknowledges that they hurt you, something they need to know. Ignoring the wound denies the weapon and allows offenders to repeat destructive patterns.[5]

## Reconciliation

Our sin made us enemies of God, but through Christ's work on the cross, God reconciled us to him. Receiving Christ transforms our hostility toward God into rejoicing in Christ (see Romans 5). Christ's work of reconciliation heals relationships among men and women. In Ephesians 2:11–22 Paul describes how Christ broke down the walls that divide us. All who believe are now members together of one body, where "there is neither Jew nor Greek, slave nor free, male nor female, for you are all one in Christ Jesus" (Galatians 3:28).

Doing the work of reconciliation is much harder than theologizing about it. But Christ commands it. Committing to confession and forgiveness doesn't always lead naturally to reconciliation, which means harmony in a relationship and increased community life in groups. For example, divorced people may confess sin and forgive one another, yet never fully reconcile the relationship. (Circumstances such as abuse, incest, or adultery may make full restoration difficult or unlikely, but full confession and forgiveness can take place.)

Small groups must work at reconciliation between members because the community quotient of the entire group is at stake. Just as in a family, rifts between members can affect the entire small group. Reconciliation means group harmony and committing to a group life that transcends individual wounds.

## The Other Side of Conflict Is Love

I (Bill) spoke to British group leaders about group conflict. A pastor asked for permission to tell a story about a Willow Creek group he had visited. Here is the gist of his story.

"I visited a couples home group where the leader was encouraging each person to become a participating member at Willow Creek. He described it as a serious commitment and asked each person to take home the membership materials—a booklet and cassette tape. The membership process had been redesigned and a new approach had been developed. Everyone was eager to see the materials and committed to start working through them, suggesting that they all do it as a group. Except for one man. Though his wife was eager to proceed, he was genuinely frustrated and did not want to become a member. And he certainly did not want the group to lay aside their present curriculum to study the membership materials.

"A minor conflict ensued. Half the group defended him; the other half wondered why he was being divisive and uncooperative. Emotions flared. What happened next was amazing. The leader couple asked people to pause and reflect for a moment, to seek God and to listen. They laid ground rules for discussion, then affirmed the man, reminding him that he was loved by the group. They told him that his contribution to the group was more important than he could ever imagine.

"One by one each member softened. People began making observations about his life and his feelings. 'It seems like this is a hard thing for you.' 'It sounds like you might need some time to process this more.' They asked questions to understand his perspective, and they committed to support and respect him. The group understood that this man was more important to God than their agenda, and they agreed to process this further."

This group understood that the other side of conflict is love. A desire to be right can easily overcome the command to love. Unchecked egos and selfish personal agendas tear at the flesh of community like wild animals devouring their fallen prey. Love, the purest of all virtues, holds these attacking beasts at bay, giving grace and freedom to the one who feels weak and vulnerable in our midst.

Pursuing God-honoring relationships within the context of timeless truth will inevitably produce healthy conflict. Love demands that we confront sin and restore relational breakdown. Communities characterized by submission to the Word of God and the practice of love will meet such conflict with grace and skill. It will be difficult; it will demand sacrifice and resolve; it will take time and sometimes tears. But we can guarantee it will be the most fruitful work you do together.

This work will help your group develop the fourth major component of small group community—well-balanced shepherding. In the next chapter we will explain how to nurture both care and growth, how groups can make disciples *and* support one another.

# Small Groups Provide Well-Balanced Shepherding

*Where are the spiritual leaders, the shepherds of the flock, the elders of God's people? Why are one or two official Christian leaders assigned the job of pastor and expected to carry a burden that belongs on many shoulders? Where are the people who can listen well and guide us through our problems to the Father's heart and who regard it as their calling to do so? Whatever became of the idea that all believers are priests?*

LARRY CRABB, CONNECTING

We still remember trying to sell dyed-in-the-wool discipleship small group leaders on their new role and ministry description in a church of small groups—shepherding. It was 1992, and most of us were new to the staff, while many of the leaders had been discipling small groups for years. Frustrated yet respectful, one leader said, "We used to talk about discipling people; now it seems we just want to shepherd them!" Heads nodded emphatically.

We could hear the group thinking, "What's it going to be? Discipleship or shepherding?" Our next words would win them to the cause or alienate them from our leadership or even from the church.

Rather than answer, we asked the small group leader who voiced his concern to describe his understanding of shepherding. "Shepherding means praying for people, helping them when they're sick, and caring for them. That sort of thing."

Our response stunned him when we affirmed, "Then if all we do is shepherd people, we are in big trouble." Again, many heads nodded.

"Unless," one of us added, "you shepherd people the way Jesus did." You can still hear the echoes of the silence today. No one moved. Every eye remained fixed on us, but this time backed up by a spirit that said, "Teach us"—and teach we did.

As we examined what the Scriptures say about shepherding, the small group leaders began to see that they had drifted into a false dichotomy. A weak view of shepherding led them to believe that when you shepherd someone, you don't develop them. They had been looking at our established discipleship groups as spiritual Green Berets, an elite military force that ate nails for breakfast, took no prisoners, and sacrificed their own lives while accomplishing the mission. They thought of the new shepherding-and-community model as something for those not yet ready for true discipleship—like army support personnel who need three squares, a warm bed, and a clean uniform.

Gradually they came to see that the Bible describes both caring and discipling as subsets of shepherding the body of Christ. They caught on to shepherding more quickly than I (Bill) had. My wake-up call came during seminary, when I worked part-time for a church. I dropped by the home of two kids in my youth group. Their father, who volunteered as the church Christian education director, ran a small farm. The kids were on an errand, so Tom invited me to help with chores.

"Sure!" I said. I was well equipped for farming work, having grown up in a Philadelphia brick row home where our front lawn was the size of a welcome mat.

"You can help me bale hay," Tom said.

"I don't do hay," I responded. "I have hay fever and a bad back from some college football injuries."

Tom, who stood 5'4", threw a fifty-pound bale over his shoulder and gazed unimpressed at my 6'2" frame. "Okay, then. You can finish milking the cows I didn't get to this morning."

Milking cows, I soon learned, meant touching them. I had seen movies where men grabbed those things hanging down from cows and pulled on them. I was not sure God wanted people to do this. I said, "I'm in seminary, so I don't think I can touch that." Tom was "utterly" amazed with my x-rated view of milking.

Finally, he asked if I could help call in the sheep. I enthusiastically agreed. Sheep-calling was like preaching. We stood at the pasture fence, watching twenty-five sheep graze. "Go ahead," he dared me. "Call them in."

"What do you say?" I asked.

"I just say, 'Hey, sheep! C'mon in!'" No sweat, I thought. A city kid with a bad back and hay fever could do this. I began in a normal speaking voice, but Tom interrupted: "You are seventy-five yards away, down wind, and they have their backs to you. Yell! Use your diaphragm, like they teach you in preaching class."

So I took a deep breath and put every inch of stomach muscle into a yell that revival preachers around the world would envy. "Hey, sheep! C'mon in!" The blessed creatures didn't move an inch. None even turned an ear.

Tom smiled sarcastically. "Do they teach you the Bible in that seminary? Have you ever read, 'My sheep hear my voice, and I know them and they follow me'?" Raising his voice only slightly, he said, "Hey, sheep! C'mon in!" All twenty-five sheep turned and ambled toward us. Tom seized this teachable moment. "Now don't you ever forget," he said. "You are the shepherd to my kids."

Suddenly, those cows looked real good. Sheepishly I answered, "I won't forget." In five minutes, Tom taught me what I had yet to learn in graduate school. Your flock had better know the voice of their shepherd. And you had better really know them—their fears, hopes, dreams, challenges.

Tom's living illustration helped Jesus' words sink in and take root in me. That episode drove me to research effective, God-honoring shepherding in the Bible. I discovered that shepherding means both supplying people's needs (care) and developing them (discipleship). We will look at the biblical picture of a shepherd, then offer practical suggestions for providing care and discipling within small groups.

## The Shepherd God Uses

Psalm 23 describes the feelings—comfort, blessing, security, hope—of being well shepherded. We must also read this psalm through the eyes of our own leadership. How would our sheep describe us as shepherds? One of our key leaders, Frank, is the epitome of Psalm 23. He tends to a small group division in the couples ministry comprising about forty-five groups and about eighty leaders. Frank is developing his leaders, "leading" them to rest and "guiding" them "in paths of righteousness"—that is, helping them grow in faith and move to new levels of maturity in Christ. They, in turn, do the same for their groups.

Psalm 23 also teaches Frank that he's obligated to care for his leaders, many of whom are older and are experiencing illness or death in their
families. As a good shepherd, he also "restores the soul." Broken, hurting, weary people need to be restored. Frank's job is to care for his front-
line leaders so that they can do the same for the hundreds of members in
their flocks. And he does it well.

Ezekiel 34 gives both the "how not to" and "how to" pictures of
shepherding. God has reserved some of his most stinging rebukes for abusive shepherds, those "who only take care of themselves" and who rule
"harshly and brutally" (Ezekiel 34:1–10). Angry and frustrated with
Israel's abusive leaders, God declares himself the shepherd in their stead:
"I myself will search for my sheep and look after them" (Ezekiel 34:11).
Verses 12–31 explain that good shepherds feed the flock with truth, lead
them to rest, search for the lost, bind up the wounded, bring back the
strays, and tend to the sick.

Ezekiel depicted a full-orbed role of shepherding that includes both
care and discipling. This "job description" can feel overwhelming to a
small group leader. The good news is that Willow Creek shepherds do not
shepherd alone. Later in this chapter we will describe how mutual ministry helps leaders shepherd their groups.

Christ describes how good shepherds express their love for the sheep
they know so well: "I am the good shepherd. The good shepherd lays
down his life for the sheep. . . . I am the good shepherd; I know my sheep
and my sheep know me—just as the Father knows me and I know the
Father—and I lay down my life for the sheep" (John 10:11–15).

Jesus knew his sheep and wanted to be known by them. He must
have been disappointed when, on the eve of his crucifixion, Philip said,
"Lord, show us the Father and that will be enough for us" (John 14:8).
Jesus' answer was more than an apologetic for his deity. You can almost
hear his heart break: "Don't you know me, Philip, even after I have been
among you such a long time?" (John 14:9).

Shepherds are servants who make sacrifices for those under their
care. Willow Creek small group leaders and coaches mow others' lawns,
care for their children, provide transportation, and readjust personal
schedules to meet the needs of their flocks. Recently, a leader phoned a
group member for a routine "check-in" call. When asked, "How are you
doing?" the woman replied, in a wan voice, "Fine."

"Really?" the leader asked.

"Well, my husband and I were hoping for a date night, the first since we had our baby four weeks ago. But the sitter just canceled. At 6 o'clock on a Friday night finding another is next to impossible, so we'll just hang out here."

It would have been appropriate for this leader to empathize and to offer comfort and prayer, then wish them a good evening. After all, she had a family, too. Instead she said, "I'll be over in thirty minutes. You guys get ready to go out. I can cover for a couple hours so you can have some time together." Do you think this leader has attendance problems in her group? Probably not. If this reflects the way she tends her flock, the sheep will eagerly seek to be shepherded.

The way leaders shepherd their small groups is a measure of their love for and understanding of the Good Shepherd. Peter denied Christ three times and returned to fishing; yet, Jesus graciously reinstated him to the community and to pastoral leadership, explaining that Peter could show his love for Jesus by feeding his sheep (John 21:15–19). Henri Nouwen wrote:

> As Jesus ministers, so he wants us to minister. He wants Peter to feed
> his sheep and care for them, not as "professionals" who know their
> clients' problems and take care of them, but as vulnerable brothers
> and sisters who know and are known, who care and are cared for,
> who forgive and are being forgiven, who love and are being loved.[1]

Notice that feeding Jesus' sheep ranks at the top of his kingdom ministry list. It grieves us when people say, "I *just* lead a small group." Leading a small group means being entrusted with an incredible ministry. We can still hear the echoes of poignant words that Bill Hybels, our senior pastor, has challenged us with through the years:

> Of all the things Jesus could have said concerning Peter's min-
> istry, he said, "Tend my sheep." He told Peter to get some people and
> train them up in the school of life, to nurture them, and to guide them.
> Jesus made time in his life to tend a little flock. And if he were here
> today, above all else, he would make time to tend a little flock. So, if
> you are a small group leader, or the leader of leaders, and you are
> making time to tend a little flock, you are doing Jesus' work. Any
> time you wonder whether you are having any impact in the kingdom,
> remember that tending a flock reflects the very heart of God and his
> plan of redemption for the world.

Peter learned about servanthood from Christ. Years later, having grasped the primacy of Christ's call to shepherd, Peter exhorted elders: "Be shepherds of God's flock that is under your care, serving as over-seers—not because you must, but because you are willing, as God wants you to be; not greedy for money, but eager to serve; not lording it over those entrusted to you, but being examples to the flock" (1 Peter 5:2–3).

At Willow Creek, even our elders function as a small group, a serving group that gathers to perform a task but also pursues community together. This passage shapes the nature and content of their communication, their approach to conflict, the process by which they make decisions, and the manner in which they relate to staff and others. They are model shepherds, as are our small group leaders.

Peter knew that anyone not willing to serve is not fit to lead. Being a small group leader takes courage and soul searching, diligence and service, character and sweat. Peter also knew the payoff: "And when the Chief Shepherd appears, you will receive the crown of glory that will never fade away" (1 Peter 5:4).

Passages throughout the Bible describe every kind of leader— prophet, priest, judge, king, apostle, elder—as having some form of shepherding responsibility. Jacob referred to "the God who has been my shepherd" (Genesis 48:15) and "the Shepherd, the Rock of Israel" (Genesis 49:24). But how can we ask human shepherds to follow the example of the Good Shepherd—without overwhelming them? The next section tells how to achieve balance between care and discipling and balance in who does what.

## The Shepherding Challenge: Balancing Care and Discipling

It is clear from the Scripture that shepherds provide care. Hurting people must be supported, prayed with, and encouraged. Groups must take responsibility for one another in community. Families need support, the sick need company, and the poor need provision. It is equally true that discipleship is required, so that people move toward full devotion to Christ.

Group leaders tend to lean into their strengths, favoring discipleship or caring, depending on gifts and personality. Here is where the danger arises. Emphasizing one without the other distorts the shepherding function God demands. It is best illustrated with this chart.

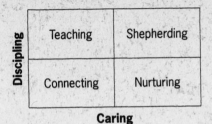

Groups that focus mainly on discipling become "teaching" groups (upper left quadrant). Members set objectives, memorize Scripture, study key doctrines, and make commitments to grow. But they don't know how to care for someone who suffers marital discord, serious illness, or job loss.

In groups that neglect both discipleship and care giving (lower left quadrant), people feel connected, have fun planning activities, and welcome newcomers. But they don't build relationships deep enough to sustain community, and they have little or no direction. When groups focus mainly on caring, people feel loved and nurtureded but are rarely challenged toward spiritual growth (lower right quadrant).

Well-balanced shepherding takes place when caring and discipling get equal emphasis in group life. It is a "both-and" proposition versus an "either-or" decision. Let's begin by discussing the "care" component and then move to the discipling function.

Small groups function much like a hospital. They provide emergency care, rehabilitative care, long-term care, and wellness care.

## Emergency Room Care: Responding to a Crisis

Your group cannot predict which crises will affect its members. Accidents happen, illnesses attack, jobs are lost, friends and family members die, and emotional trauma strikes one or more members at any given time. But your group can commit to providing emergency care.

While leading a small groups conference in Australia, I (Bill) heard a remarkable story. A participant explained that a man in her group had suffered a heart attack. "His wife made two phone calls—an emergency call for an ambulance and a call to our small group leader." She paused, and then with a big grin exclaimed, "The small group was the first to arrive!"

We have seen this story repeated a thousand times in our church. Group members are often the first to be contacted in a crisis and are often the first to lend a hand. They visit hospitals, cook meals, clean up flooded houses, pray with downsized employees, recharge dead car batteries, and give money when needed. No single individual could provide all these services. It is the privilege of the small group community.

Paul said, "Carry each other's burdens, and in this way you will fulfill the law of Christ" (Galatians 6:2). We carry each other's heavy load in community and thus lighten the burden. You may feel confused, then, when Paul says a few sentences later, that "each one should carry his own load" (Galatians 6:5). But the word he uses for "burden" (v. 2) means something heavy, like a boulder. The word he uses for "load" (v. 5) means something light, like a small backpack. He's saying that we should help carry one another's boulders, but each of us should carry our own backpacks.

As leaders guide a group to become a hospital for healing, members will take turns bearing burdens. Leaders don't have to shoulder the pain of each member. Emergencies are natural times to achieve the goal of mutual care-giving. Church members outside your small group will likely respond to a crisis within your group, such as a house burning down or a death in the family. But the care you receive from someone in your little community will probably matter most. It will also likely continue for longer than care provided by casual acquaintances.

### Rehabilitative Care: Helping with Recovery

Small groups are uniquely suited to provide follow-up care after the crisis has ended. Steve, a husband in a couples group, watched for four months as his father succumbed to a severe illness. His wife and kids accompanied him almost weekly on the four-hundred-mile trip to Michigan, where his dad suffered at home. In the final weeks he sought to lead his dad to Christ. Yet his father gave no indication of responding to the gospel.

Many came to the funeral, and many came to Steve's home for a week or two afterward. But they weren't close to Steve and didn't stay in touch. They weren't there for his first Christmas or Easter without his dad. They didn't know his dad's birthday. They weren't around to hear Steve's small children ask, "Where is Grandpa?" Acquaintances and distant family members had no clue when Steve confronted painful memories of his father's death. It wasn't their fault; that's just reality. Most people could provide only immediate support—Steve's small group could do more.

Though support may also be required from counselors, therapists, or doctors, small groups can provide consistent love and care for people recovering from tragedy. Months after his dad's death, Steve's small group members were still praying for him, meeting with him at home or work, and encouraging him at meetings. Each time the group gathered, they could devote some time to his needs.

## Long-Term Care: A Lifetime of Support

One Willow Creek small group is filled with people in chronic emotional or physical pain. One member has liver cancer, another lost her husband to a brain tumor, a third often suffers depression, while yet another lost an adult daughter, brutally murdered in Chicago. Pain creates a certain partnership among sufferers. Any doubt concerning this truth will vanish when you visit a meeting of Alcoholics Anonymous or a grief support group. Some of these group members remain friends for a lifetime, even after they have overcome the condition that drove them to the group. They form deep bonds and build community, perhaps because it's often easier to find community in pain or failure than in pleasure or success. As Parker Palmer explains:

> The nonmonstrous parts of ourselves, the parts we consider angelic, are parts that separate us from others; they make for distinction, not unity. These parts give us pride because they make us different, not because they unite us with the common lot of humankind. Our successes and our glories are not the stuff of community, but our sins and failures are. In those difficult areas of our lives we confront the human condition, and we begin to learn compassion for all beings who share the limits of life itself.[2]

*Sharing the limits of life.* We all have limitations to a varying degree. All of us require care for a season, yet almost every small group has one or two people whose obstacles will follow them to the grave. For whatever reason, they will never fully recover from their emotional or physical wounds. In *The Coming Church Revolution*, consultant Carl George identifies these folks as "extra care required persons."

No one person has the resources to single-handedly provide long-term care to another person. But with help from other support systems, groups can provide a lifetime of encouragement, prayer, and love to those who require extra care. Each little community will share some of the burden and ease some of the suffering, uniting in love with the one who has need.

In the Jerusalem church, a group of Greek-speaking Jewish widows was missing out on the daily food distribution. Truly these women required extra care and support. The Twelve formed a ministry team of Greek men "full of the Spirit and wisdom" (Acts 6:3) to meet the widows' short- and long-term needs. Their support freed the apostles to concentrate on preaching and prayer.

## Wellness Care: Mutual Support

When Jesus speaks about shepherding, he does not want us to think about a brave, lonely shepherd who takes care of a large flock of obedient sheep. In many ways, he makes it clear that ministry is a communal and mutual experience.... Indeed, whenever we minister together, it is easier for people to recognize that we do not come in our own name, but in the name of the Lord Jesus who sent us.[3]

HENRI NOUWEN

Many of us, like Nouwen, were taught to do ministry alone. Members expected us to be a pastoral version of Superman. (Incidentally, he never really worked alone. Without Jimmy Olson or Lois Lane he'd be pushing up daisies in a field of kryptonite.) Unfortunately, the church has tended to model ministry more on Superman than Jesus, expecting one man—courageous, seminary-equipped, all-knowing—to minister alone. "Faster than a speeding nursery worker, more powerful than the stewardship committee, able to fill the baptismal font from a single bucket, it's Super Pastor! Teaching, preaching, visiting, counseling, praying, visiting, meeting with boards, speaking at picnics, visiting, singing in the choir—that's what we pay him for. Stand in awe as we watch him pour himself out like a drink offering on the altar of the church! Go pastor; you're our man; if you can't do it, no one can!"

Small groups can make the same error. They sometimes expect their leader to respond to every need, teach lessons, personally disciple each member, make all phone calls, pray for the sick, counsel members back from despair, and make every meeting an adventure. "Here comes Super Leader! Watch her go! She intercedes around the clock, prepares for meetings eight weeks in advance, personally visits each member daily, and plans the group calendar for the next four years!" Martha Stewart would be proud. The group loves her. Too bad she only lasts six months.

Yes, groups need discipling *and* caring. But one person cannot adequately accomplish both. That's why leaders often neglect one emphasis. Mutual ministry is the only way for a group to experience both care and discipling. Mutual ministry was God's design from the beginning. God never intended for a select few to minister to many. God envisioned a community approach to shared ministry, so all could participate and none would be neglected. Gilbert Bilezikian cites the creation narrative as an example of God's design.

> At least three lessons can be drawn about the nature of ministry from the story of beginnings. First, in the divine order of things, the making of community requires work. Community does not just happen. Second, the members of community are servants together under divine authority. They are all "ministers"—a term derived from a Latin word that means "servant." Third, the work of community requires the total involvement of its members. No one is excluded or excused from contributing, out of one's abilities, to the common tasks.[4]

Now let's look at how groups, guided by leaders, can work together to disciple one another.

### Discipling: Intentional Modeling

A recent news vignette showed police pursuing a government employee—who was driving a stolen U.S. Army tank. At speeds of forty to fifty miles per hour, he raced through inner-city streets, flattening cars, terrifying pedestrians, smashing into buildings, and toppling traffic signs. Finally, while trying to cross a major highway, he got hung up on the median wall. Police surrounded the tank and apprehended the suspect. The police worked hard to catch him, because the stakes were high and the situation was urgent.

What would it be like if we pursued Jesus Christ with the same urgency and attention? What would it be like if we got serious about the life that Jesus wants us to live? People desperately need leaders who model the life of Jesus Christ and intentionally move others toward the same goal of Christlikeness.

Paul advised, "Follow my example as I follow the example of Christ" (1 Corinthians 11:1). He told the Thessalonians that he, Silas, and Timothy supported themselves by making tents "in order to make ourselves a model for you to follow" (2 Thessalonians 3:9). Very interesting. Leaders show others the way but are not expected to walk the path for them. Each of us must take responsibility for that. But often it still requires a leader to model the life of Christ.

Because I (Russ) oversee several people who are already mature Christians, I have to focus enormous time and energy on modeling Christ for them. To shepherd these folks has been the most challenging and enriching addition to my spiritual life. I know that unless I model those things that may inspire them to the next level of spiritual development, I am not serving them well. Unless they see God's ongoing work in my character, I am not doing all I can to disciple them toward spiritual transformation.

Joe Stowell, president of Moody Bible Institute, once told us, "It takes a changing life to change a life." Until you understand how changing your life can change another person's life, you won't be a full-orbed shepherd. One of the best ways to become a better shepherd is to spend more time with Christ. Make yourself available to God through the Holy Spirit to change your life.

### Discipling: Intentional Shepherding

We used to spend a lot of time with our leaders repeating, "Life change, life change, life change." We next tried to clarify our guidance by speaking instead about "spiritual formation" or "spiritual transformation." Paul talked about laboring for the church "until Christ is formed in you" (Galatians 4:19). Our Willow Creek mission statement says that we aim to "turn irreligious people into fully devoted followers of Christ." Finally, we developed a framework to give people a better idea of what it means to develop Christlikeness—that is, to become fully devoted to Christ. We call our discipleship framework "The Five Gs." These five words or phrases help people measure their spiritual progress:

#### Grace

We want people to experience saving grace, understand its full measure, and then extend it to others. Grace means coming to grips with our sin before a holy God and receiving Christ's substitutionary work on our behalf. When groups truly understand how amazing God's grace is, their hearts fill with love for those who have not yet experienced it.

### Growth

In order to achieve maturity, groups must commit themselves to those practices, relationships, and experiences that will bring them into the presence of Christ and transform them into his image. Practicing spiritual disciplines both on your own and as a group will ignite your group toward greater spiritual growth and power.

### Groups

We refer here to the value of community in both small groups and the larger group, as experienced through corporate worship. People need to participate at both group levels to truly connect with Christ and one another. It is exciting to see many group members sitting together in church, taking classes and serving together. They are as committed to the larger community as they are to their small group.

### Gifts

As Christ followers we respond to the Holy Spirit's work in our lives and, as we grow, start to give something back to the body. Paul discussed this kind of servanthood in 1 Corinthians 12. God rejoices when his followers use their spiritual gifts so serve the kingdom and minister to those outside the church.

### Good Stewardship

Eventually we grow enough to share not just what we *have* but all of who we *are*—our time, talents, treasure, and even our lives. As Paul said in 1 Thessalonians 2:8, "We loved you so much that we were delighted to share with you not only the gospel of God but our lives as well, because you had become so dear to us." Groups that practice good stewardship remember Christ's blessings in their own lives and eagerly share them with others. They share themselves not only in their own church but anywhere they can meet a need—locally, nationally, and internationally.

We have aligned our participating membership process with the Five Gs. So, when someone asks to become a participating member, they go through a process of studying each "G" in the Bible and committing to it. Leaders encourage group members to commit to all Five Gs and become participating church members. Because increasing numbers of small group participants are discipled toward church membership, the discipling process becomes mutual. The leader guides the process, but as each individual commits to grow, everyone encourages each other. Community-based transformation becomes a group effort.

Our "Shepherding Plan" is another tool that helps people continue spiritual growth long after they have joined the church. (*Leading Life-Changing Small Groups* includes a version of this plan.) The Shepherding Plan helps leaders take a Five Gs inventory of each member. Leaders help members build relationships, discern spiritual needs, and develop a plan for growth. The Five Gs rubric helps each group discuss and assess spiritual growth on a quarterly basis.

I (Russ) have used this plan with people at Willow Creek and at other churches where Bill and I teach and consult. In one church I asked the people to pair up and use this plan to discuss their spiritual lives. I noticed two men in intense conversation, so I asked their opinion of the process. One man responded, "You know, we have been involved in ministry leadership together for three years, and I just learned more in six or seven minutes about my friend here than I discovered in the previous three years!" It's amazing what a question can do.

Not everyone uses the Shepherding Plan in a structured way. Some leaders simply have it in their heads and apply it more intuitively. Either way, the Five Gs and Shepherding Plan offer a grid or framework to prod group members toward growth. Whether you use our tools, adapt someone else's framework, or create your own, you will find it's invaluable to choose a set of spiritual goals for intentional application.

Let's be clear, however. A shepherd cannot truly disciple without a definitive, mutually agreed-on set of spiritual goals. Don't let this slide. Incomplete descriptions of spiritual growth or a litany of Bible verses will not produce the spiritual growth you seek. But if you do the hard work of creating a framework, then training leaders to use it, you will achieve mutual ministry guided by disciple-making leaders. You'll be glad you made the effort—and so will they.

## Maintaining the Balance

Whether you shepherd a highly specialized group or a mainstream small group, you'll need to care for and make disciples of every member. This balanced shepherding can only happen when your group members embrace mutual ministry to one another under your capable leadership.

Once people begin to grow in Christ and understand their responsibilities to the body, care will begin to flow from one member to another. When groups get enmeshed with a single member's needs, leaders must lovingly and directly call the group toward spiritual growth. Likewise, when groups focus so much on teaching and discipleship goals that they neglect other needs, leaders must reestablish caring processes.

■

Practicing community in small groups begins with authentic relationships. When members are known, loved, served, celebrated, and admonished, they begin to change. Timeless scriptural truth meets authentic life as leaders ask questions and design meetings to produce holy moments, evidences of God's presence and power. As community develops and God's truth meets sinners' lives, conflict will result. Wise leaders will help maturing groups use conflict to grow, individually and together, more like Christ. Finally, a spirit of mutual ministry will develop among members as they promote discipleship and provide care.

Community building is an act of love. Ultimately and supremely community means the giving of our lives to one another—no more, no less.

> The real question is not, "What can we offer each other?" but "Who can we be for each other?" No doubt it is wonderful when we can repair something for a neighbor, give helpful advice to a friend, offer wise counsel to a colleague, bring healing to a patient, or announce good news to a parishioner, but there is a greater gift than all of this. It is the gift of our own life that shines through all we do. As I grow older, I discover more and more that the greatest gift I have to offer is my own joy of living, my own inner peace, my own sense of well-being. When I ask myself, "Who helps me most?" I must answer, "The one who is willing to share his or her life with me."[5]

A church built on small groups will become a community that can reach a wider community. This is God's will for his people. This is our privilege as leaders. This is worth giving ourselves to—one life at a time.

# DEVELOPING LEADERS OF SMALL GROUPS

Part 3

During a break at a small groups conference where I (Bill) was speaking, I heard two tragic stories within ten minutes of each other. Two small group pastors shared similar experiences. Two years earlier, they had started small groups in their churches. As they cast a vision for small group life, people got excited. Each church started about two dozen groups in the first year. The pastors encouraged all church members to join small groups, and their ministries skyrocketed. However, a year later each church had only three groups left. The pastors were asking themselves, "What did we do wrong? Will we be able to recover? Do small groups really work?"

My heart sank when I heard their stories. A few questions revealed why they had failed. I asked these two pastors:

- How much time was spent creating your leadership development process?
- Were these leaders properly coached and supported?
- What events did you use to inspire and encourage them along the way?
- Did the senior leadership of the church model effective small group leadership to these rising new leaders?
- What training resources were available to them?

These and other questions revealed that these pastors were so eager to start small groups that they skipped a vital step. They began the groups without creating a leadership structure to support those groups. In small group ministry, speed often kills. Better to have a few quality groups with emerging, well-trained leaders who will reproduce themselves for a lifetime than to have twenty small groups start next week but disappear in six months.

An emerging small group ministry cannot succeed without a commitment to effective leadership deployment. In this section, we will focus on how to identify and recruit small group leaders (chapter 8), train them for effective service (chapter 9), then coach and support them so their service is long term (chapter 10). Once a church achieves these goals, it really has recreated itself.

# 8

# Enlisting Small Group Leaders

*The church is the hope of the world, and its future rests in the hands of its leaders.*

BILL HYBELS

The small group ministry in a church rises and falls on the quality of its leaders. Envisioned, equipped, and compassionate leaders will guide a group toward spiritual growth, mutual care, and Spirit-empowered service. Godly leaders will facilitate the development of authentic relationships and create places in small groups where truth meets life. But how do you identify and recruit such leaders?

Over the course of their Willow Creek journey, Bob and Marie have led many kinds of groups. Spend five minutes with them and you will understand why people follow them and submit to their servant leadership. They challenge people who are adrift spiritually, rebuke those who pursue sinful behavior, teach people with encouraging words from Scripture, love those who need support, and challenge future leaders to exercise their leadership gifts and potential.

For years now, they have been coaches—our Willow Creek term for shepherds of other small group leaders. Most exciting is that Bob and Marie are in their seventies yet continue to be an example to the flock. We have watched them negotiate life-threatening illnesses, medical challenges, family disappointments, and personal spiritual battles. Even amid trials, they seek to walk with God and reflect his character. This is why people follow Bob and Marie.

The future of your small group ministry rests on your leaders' shoulders. Every church (including ours) would love to have hundreds of leaders like Bob and Marie, but that means building a leadership corps must become a top priority. The first step is to identify and recruit small group leaders.

## Identifying Small Group Leaders

When you first begin developing small groups, identifying leaders is as easy as shaking a tree of ripe fruit. Your church probably has a pool of experienced people who have proven themselves in other ministries. You simply need to give them a vision for small group life and nudge them to consider a new role—small group leader.

The challenge comes when your church moves into a more developmental phase. You need to do more than motivate proven leaders. You must produce new ones. First, know what you are looking for. People suited for small group leadership share certain core characteristics. Second, focus on looking for people with these core characteristics rather than limiting your search to confident extroverts—the types often described as "natural leaders."

### Look at Who They "A. R. E."

A simple acrostic—Affections, Reputation, Expectations—describes the essential characteristics for small group leadership. Affections are those things we love most. Reputation, what other people say about someone, matters. People suited for small group leadership will share your church's expectations for service.

#### Affections

Margaret Guenther defines affections in her book *The Practice of Prayer*:

> Whatever its characteristics, every one of us has a spirituality, what Augustine called an *ordo amorie*, an ordering of our loves. What do we most cherish? What do we most desire? What is the treasure hidden in the core of our being? Our spirituality is not what we profess to believe, but how we order our loves.[1]

People suited to leadership love God, people, truth, and the church. The greatest gifts a leader can give a small group are a relationship with Christ and the passion to become more like him. Small group leaders pursue Christlikeness so they can set an example for the flock. But even more important, their love of God connects them to the only true source of spiritual life.

Whether a leader is an introvert or an extrovert, he or she must have a basic love and affection for people. You cannot develop authentic relationships without loving people, whether they are seekers or believers. Look for small group leaders who know that all people matter to God and who have a special place in their heart for those seeking him.

Leaders love the transforming truth of the Word of God. They saturate themselves with Scripture, reflect on it, meditate on its virtues, and seek to practice its commands. Without this love of truth, leaders won't be able to help their group members become more like Christ.

Bill Hybels has said, "There's nothing like the local church when the local church is working right." Good small group leaders see the church—the Bride of Christ—as the only means by which to accomplish the mission God has for us. They view small group leadership as a core ministry, because healthy churches are made up of little communities of faith—small groups. Potential leaders make the local church a priority and fully participate in its ministries and services.

These affections—for God, people, truth, and the church—mark a person whose heart is in line with God's heart. These four loves are like putty that can be molded into a passionate leader. They will help you identify emerging or potential leaders.

### Reputation

A person's reputation offers clues to that person's preparation for leadership. Make it a point to meet people close to the potential leader. Inquire what they think of the person's character, trustworthiness, and way of relating to others. Ask people to assess a candidate's leadership potential. Do they believe the person could grow toward leadership? Why or why not? Have they served others or the church in ways that produce effective fruits of ministry?

Any competent employer will check a potential employee's references. The church can afford to do no less. It's easy to check references if the potential leader is well known or has been around the church for some time. Sometimes, however, you will have to ask the candidate for references, probably some close friends or people they know through church.

Be sure to follow through on these references. One of our staff interviewed a potential leader who gave three references. The interviewer phoned only the first person, assuming that, since the remaining two names were other Willow Creek staff, they would endorse the candidate.

After putting the person into leadership, the interviewer got a call from one of the two staff references, who said, "I noticed you put Mike into a leadership role. I wish you had called me. He has some character issues that need work before he should be a leader." It is harder to remove a leader than to properly qualify one. Do your homework.

## Expectations

Make sure candidates understand and support expectations for service. As you discuss what senior staff, elders, or other key lay leaders expect from a small group leader, look especially for people who commit themselves to participating membership, respect spiritual authority, and pursue life-long learning.

We expect potential leaders to become fully participating members of the church. This functions as both a discipleship and a screening process. As people go through the membership curriculum and affirmation process at Willow Creek, we get a good look at their spiritual condition and willingness to grow. Since we expect potential leaders to be people who are growing in their love for God and the church, it makes sense that they would be devoted and committed enough to become church members.

When someone agrees to explore small group leadership, they place themselves under the spiritual authority of elders and experienced lay leaders. Leaders show their hearts are right when they submit themselves to people who will care for them and hold them accountable to mutual objectives and spiritual growth. Never give spiritual authority to a person who will not submit to spiritual authority.

"All learning," someone said, "is the result of failed expectations." Leading a small group is a constant and challenging adventure, filled with failed expectations. Among other skills, leaders must grow in the ability to relate to people, manage conflict, understand more of the Word of God, impart vision, respond to people in need, and raise up future leaders. Therefore, life-long learning is mandatory. You have to seek training in your areas of need or weakness.

## Looking for Leaders in All the Right Places

Where do you find leaders? This is a trick question. Rather than look for *leaders*, we encourage churches to look for *people*. There's always a greater supply of people than of obvious leaders. Some leaders emerge through a surprising mix of circumstances.

I (Bill) was leading a couples group with Gail, my wife, when a new couple joined. The wife was warm, talkative, easy to relate to. The husband (I'll call him "Stan") was quiet. For the first few months he spoke infrequently and usually not very long. He was sincere but shy. Once he told us it was difficult for him to move quickly into group relationships because he feared being the center of attention. "I was talking to a coworker at the water cooler, when suddenly I noticed lots of other people looking at me. I was petrified. I hate it when I am speaking and a group is staring at me," he said.

I listened to Stan and thought to myself, "Scratch this guy off the potential small group leaders list." A few months later, after attending a Promise Keepers Men's Conference, several of us decided to start a men's group for accountability and encouragement as fathers and husbands. We didn't want to interfere with family time, so we decided to meet on Tuesdays before work for an hour of prayer, study, and mutual edification. Stan and I were in the group, but we had no leader. Since Gail and I were already leading the couples group, I had no desire to lead this group. I asked, "Who would like to lead?" These wise, strong, brave men, having just returned from a men's conference, eagerly said, "Not me." I suggested that we rotate leadership each week until someone felt comfortable to permanently lead the group.

When it was Stan's turn, he shocked us. After preparing for three hours, he led a half-hour discussion that was a veritable clinic on how to lead a small group. His questions were probing, his feedback encouraging, and his insight into people's lives profound. He guided us through a lively discussion that had both depth and a call to action. He made comments like, "Dan, I hear what you're saying, but I wonder if there's something deeper that you really want to express. I feel like you are holding back." Once he asked us all to stop, lay hands on, and pray for a man with a work crisis.

I phoned him after the meeting to ask how it felt to lead. "Not bad," he said. Not bad! It was the best small group we'd had in months. The next Tuesday we unanimously elected Stan as our leader. I would have never chosen Stan. But God saw something in Stan that I could not. When given the opportunity to lead in the context of safe relationships, Stan rose to the occasion.

So where do you find leaders? Sometimes right under your nose. You find them in small groups, Sunday school classes, committees, service activities, and church-wide events. But you might not identify them at first. Ask God to help you recognize leaders emerging from the right mix of relationships, ministry opportunities, and time. Stop looking for leaders and start developing people.

## Recruiting Small Group Leaders

Many pastors are good at "announcing" but less proficient at "recruiting." Recruiting requires intention, meeting personally with potential leaders, and calling them to a new kind of life.

It has been said that much of Christianity is about leaving. Abraham left his home when God called him to a new land. Men and women leave their birth families and cleave to a spouse. Jesus Christ calls us to leave behind the things of this world and take up our cross. Similarly, recruiting means asking people to leave behind some of what they now do and make time for leadership development.

### Making the Ask

Since most people believe they have no extra time, few will respond to an announcement asking for volunteer leaders. That's why you need to call them to a vision. If you want to build a church of small groups that is led by leaders who understand the nature of their call and the value of their service, you will need to specifically "make the ask." This process involves announcing, envisioning, inviting, and challenging. Some people will respond at each level. The more focused and personal you become, the more leaders you will recruit.

Public announcements are the first step in calling people to small group leadership. Staff leaders describe the concept of emerging small group ministry and leadership. Sometimes they do this through a brochure or letter. A few people will respond to this level of call. Most, however, will receive the announcement as information, not as a personal call to commitment.

The next step is casting a vision for leadership in the church. A leader passionately explains this vision for new ministry and describes how leaders can make a difference in the church and the world. The leader casts a bold vision for what the church would look like if everyone were shepherded appropriately. This envisioning step will inspire some people to indicate further interest by filling out a response card or sign-up sheet.

An invitation takes things to the next level. You've publicly announced the ministry and described the vision. Now it's time for you personally to invite people to join you. A personal invitation is more powerful than a written one. People can see your heart and engage in dialogue as you explain why you're asking them to join you to lead the church into the future. The high-touch nature of a personal invitation usually moves many people across the line toward exploring leadership.

Strong leaders, however, often need a personal face-to-face challenge. They generally don't respond to announcements or envisioning or even personal invitations. They need someone to look them in the eye and issue a big challenge. Often these people are highly committed at work and in the community. They are already viewed as leaders. It takes a wake-up call to get their attention and let them know that this is worth giving their life to.

Each of these four "making the ask" approaches is valuable. You can combine them into more effective calls to ministry. But don't stop with the announcement or envisioning, because those steps won't be sufficient for you to inspire and motivate enough leaders.

## Reluctant Leaders Often Make the Best Leaders

Even after you complete all four steps of making the ask, some people will hold back. They are afraid, perhaps because of a poor leadership experience. Maybe someone invited them to lead but then "used" rather than empowered them. These and other factors may lead to a syndrome we call "the reluctant leader."

Like Moses, these people either feel inadequate or do not understand the nature of leadership. Like Moses, they voice multiple objections to leading. "Who me? You've got to be kidding! Who would ever follow me? What if I fail? I don't have the abilities or the skills. Are you sure you can't find someone else to do this?"

Moses, one of the first great reluctant leaders in the Bible, made all these excuses in Exodus 3 and 4. Yet God met each objection by promising his presence, power, and provision. God approached Moses and made an ask. It was no small ask—and it scared Moses. We have found that most potential small group leaders view being asked to lead a group at about the same level that Moses responded to God's invitation to lead Israel: "You have got to be kidding!"

Moses thought his speech impediment disqualified him from leadership. You'll find that some potential leaders feel similarly inadequate with regard to Bible teaching, or caring for people in pain, or praying, or a less than optimal spiritual life. Because they measure themselves against a senior pastor or popular lay leader, they feel skeptical about their own leadership potential.

How do we convince someone that, with God's help, they can lead a group? Certainly, God's direct call to Moses through divine revelation was a unique situation. This Scripture is not intended as a lesson in leadership recruitment; yet, it does offer insights into approaching reluctant leaders. Allow us to draw some parallels. If you look at how God made the ask, you will notice that he built a relationship with Moses, described a need, and then promised support, resources, and a partner for Moses to meet the need.

It's easier to recruit reluctant leaders when you have a growing relationship with them. They know your intentions, heart, and character, and they have seen you make ministry decisions and work with other people. God began a relationship with Moses so he could reveal a great plan for Israel. Calling for leaders may be viewed as simply the church asking people to participate in another program or have another meeting. But when a friend or a close relationship describes a need in the life of the Body of Christ, it feels like an invitation to participate in ministry.

"I have indeed seen the misery of my people in Egypt," said God to Moses (Exodus 3:7). God explained that the situation was urgent. We, too, must passionately and accurately explain why our churches need shepherds to guide people to spiritual transformation. Tell exactly how and why the present structure is failing to care for and develop people. Explain: "Without you, we don't think we can accomplish the purposes God has set before us in this church."

"I will be with you," says God. There's nothing more encouraging in ministry than the certainty of God's presence and power. Leadership can be lonely. You can hear Moses saying, "You want me to handle this alone? How can I begin to think about what you are asking?" Early in the conversation, God assures that he will be with Moses. We must remind our potential leaders that God will be with them, and so will we. It's not as if we're sending them off into a jungle with a machete, shouting, "Let us know how it goes!"

God gave Moses a staff and the power to do miracles. Likewise, reluctant leaders need to know they will receive the resources—curriculum, training, leadership development tools—they need to accomplish their ministry.

God softened Moses' reluctance to lead by giving him Aaron as a partner. Paul often traveled with partners like Priscilla and Aquilla; Jesus had the disciples; David had Jonathan. Every small group needs at least one partner in ministry—what we call an "apprentice." We never want leaders to lead alone. Don't call people to build a community without also building a "leadership community."

Reluctant leaders are often the best leaders. The person who has said "no" to you may be your next Moses or Esther. They cannot see in themselves what you see in them. That's why you must cast vision, remind them that you will support them, and assure them that they are desperately needed and have the leadership ability. Never let them forget that God's power and presence will make up for any perceived inadequacies. Don't let people off the hook too quickly. Never manipulate or coerce— but do challenge.

If we truly believe that someone can shepherd others in the flock, then we ought to ask and challenge them to step forward. Ultimately, however, they must sense the call of God in their own lives. We won't badger anyone or beat them into submission. But we will ask them more than once and continue to pray that God does a work in their lives. If ultimately they see and sense this, they will respond and join us in the great adventure.

### Assessing Those Eager to Lead

Many potential leaders are reluctant. However, some people have been waiting for you to tap them on the shoulder. They reply, "I thought you'd never ask!" In assessing people eager to lead, remember that the motives for leadership are more important than the skills required to lead a group. It's also much easier to interview a potential leader properly than it is to remove a bad one. Here are some cautions to keep in mind when you speak with people who are eager to lead.

It's not unusual to find that highly energetic people start a group, then come and tell you they have one going. "What should I do next?" they ask. These go-getters usually turn out to be fine. Many have been overlooked or did not have an opportunity to use their leadership abilities in other ministry settings. Finally, they hear you describe small group leadership and are excited to participate. If the eagerness is appropriate and the potential leader proves to be spiritually sound and ready for leadership, then they simply need confirmation.

Problems arise when people are eager to lead because they are trying to solve their own problems rather than shepherd others. Perhaps they want to *lead* a group because they really *need* a group. The group becomes an excuse for them to accomplish their own agenda and become the focus of attention. Be especially wary of three types of people eager to lead: those who see themselves as teachers, those who see themselves as counselors, and those who love structure. These people may turn out to be good leaders, but exercise caution when you interview and recruit them.

"Teachers" tend to teach because that's their gift and desire. A group leader who simply teaches may use the small group as a platform for sermonizing. But if this potential leader is also gifted with sensitivity and listening skills, she or he will be able to balance teaching and shepherding, to lead a group where truth meets life. Talk to others who have seen this person lead. Does she guide discussions? Is she a good listener? Does he tend to dominate conversations with little interest in learning about what others are thinking or feeling?

Counselors have a strong desire to see people's lives change. This is an honorable trait. However, the "counselor type" may view each person in the small group as a problem. Coach your leaders not to enter into a therapeutic counseling relationship with everyone in the group. Rather, the objective is to create a mutually caring environment where people support each other. Occasionally a group leader may pursue more intensive one-on-one therapeutic interactions, but most of these long-term needs should be handled by a professional.

We do not train our small group leaders to take the role of counselor. Their emphasis should be on shepherding and mutual growth in the context of community. When small group leaders take on the role of counselor, focusing especially on the one or two group members with the greatest needs, the group dynamic suffers.

Some people eager to lead simply love control. When such people sneak into small group leadership, they tend to be overly structured and critically demanding of their small group members. This type of leader seeks to coerce agreement rather than taking a collaborative approach to group ideas and feelings. Controlling leaders cannot stand dissenters.

They try to make members feel guilty for disagreeing: "Well, I guess all that hard work I did to prepare for this meeting just goes out the window." Or they laughingly dismiss other opinions: "I can't imagine anyone would think that."

Spend the time necessary with people eager to lead. Discern whether their gifts of enthusiasm, teaching, counseling, and structure are balanced by other gifts necessary to lead. If left unchecked, unbalanced tendencies can destroy community in a small group.

Once you have identified and recruited group leaders, it's time to prepare and support them. You will do this through training, coaching, and creating events that inspire your leaders.

# 9

# Training Small Group Leaders

*The two men would go to the ballpark and, as the sun climbed higher in the sky, would work for hours in the heat.... His minor league teammates—most of them more skilled than he— were still asleep or sitting by the motel pool. And he wouldn't go back to his room. Instead he [Michael Jordan] would ask [batting coach] Mike Barnett if they could work longer—if they could keep practicing in the sun.*

BOB GREENE, CHICAGO TRIBUNE

Imagine going out your front door the moment after you read this and attempting to run a marathon. There are probably a few of you who could, but most of you would not be able to complete the 26-mile, 385-yard run, no matter how hard you tried! However, if you decided that this time next year you wanted to run a marathon, you would begin training today. As John Ortberg reminds us often around Willow Creek, "Training helps us do what we cannot accomplish through sheer effort." No matter how hard a well-intentioned person tries, without training he or she will not be successful at any endeavor.

People wise in the area of spiritual formation have emphasized that training—not trying—is the key. Training means helping someone acquire a skill. It's different from development, which includes character growth, increased ministry responsibility, and nurture. While development is a long-term process of shepherding someone through the Five Gs (grace,

---

Bob Greene, *Chicago Tribune* (June 17, 1998), writing on basketball great Michael Jordan's work ethic in minor league baseball.

growth, groups, gifts, and good stewardship, as described in chapter 7), training is more focused. Small group leader training must give consideration to three key elements: training objectives and delivery, training guidelines, and the training audience.

## Clear Ministry Objectives and Creative Delivery

Small group leaders won't be effective unless they understand their role. This chart outlines a small group leader's ministry description.

|  | During Meetings | Between Meetings |
| --- | --- | --- |
| **Gather—** Invite current or potential members into community | Build intimacy, transparency, and authentic relationships in the group | Build friends with existing group members and seek to invite new ones |
| **Develop—** Take each person the next step in spiritual growth or leadership | Create a place where truth meets life | Shepherd members and develop apprentice leaders |
| **Serve—** Complete ministry tasks together | Plan and prepare for strategic serving opportunities | Serve personally outside the group or serve together as a group |

You will be most effective in training leaders in each of these skills if you use a variety of training methods. Keep your delivery creative by using classroom training, apprentice training, and on-the-job training.

### Classroom Training

Most churches resort to classroom training because it's easy to put a lot of people in a room, set up a podium, and talk to them about leadership. But this is teaching, not training. For a classroom meeting to qualify as training, leaders need a chance to break into small groups and practice the skills they've just heard about. We have had success with this formula: teach, demonstrate, practice, evaluate. Teach them about the skill, demonstrate how the skill works (either with a role play or a video clip), allow them to practice at their table, and then ask someone at the table to provide feedback. This provides a safe environment for group leaders to experiment with skills and get immediate feedback on their performance.

Skills best-suited to classroom training include listening, leading a discussion, crafting great questions, and dealing with conflict. Granted, in the real life of a small group, things may work out differently, but at least classroom practice gives people an idea of what to expect in their own small groups.

### Apprentice Training

While classroom training is content driven, apprentice training is relationally driven. Apprentice training allows a rising leader to observe a small group leader in action. It's the method we use most at Willow Creek, and you can learn more about it in our book *Leading Life-Changing Small Groups*. Basically, a leader chooses an apprentice and begins to model small group leadership to him or her. The relationship between apprentice and leader allows interaction on leadership issues and small group methods. As an apprentice gradually assumes more responsibility for leading the group, the leader provides feedback. Observing the apprentice while he or she leads a meeting helps the mentor assess the apprentice's character and spiritual growth.

### On-the-Job Training

On-the-job training simply means that leaders learn as they lead. Maturing leaders receive much of their training while leading. They experiment with new methods and try applying new skills within their group. Sometimes a coach (who shepherds small group leaders) will visit a group to give the leader more feedback and encouragement. On-the-job training can be an excellent training method for leaders who take time to reflect on their leadership and to ask for tips from group members, coaches, and others.

## Training Guidelines

After college I (Bill) took a sales position with Procter & Gamble in New York City. My territory was comprised of misfit and neglected grocery stores that existing sales reps had graciously given to me to "help get me started." Several were in the most challenging areas of Brooklyn and Queens—Bedford Stuyvesant, East New York, Flatbush Avenue. These neighborhoods were poverty ridden, graffiti-covered, and in desperate need of renovation. In some cases the streets resembled a war zone—crumbled buildings, abandoned vehicles, sidewalks strewn with trash and clutter. It was a far cry from the ivy-covered architecture and plush surroundings that epitomized the university from which I had freshly graduated. (I like to tell people that I got my degree at Princeton but my education in New York.) Now I understood why the other sales reps had eagerly donated these stores to me.

During my one-day orientation at the district office in suburban White Plains, I was told that my manager would make calls with me for the first week, visiting each of my fifty stores while demonstrating proper sales techniques. He would "pave the way" for me, acclimating me to the territory and showing me how to close a sale. Then it would be my turn, and he would coach me, evaluating my progress.

After two sales calls in some pretty tough neighborhoods we arrived at the third store. My manager said to me, "OK, now it's your turn. Go make the pitch."

I soon grasped that he was not referring to baseball. "Me? What do I say?"

He smiled. It was the kind of smile they give you at the roller coaster when they say, "Don't be afraid, it's not that high." He handed me the sales book, said a few encouraging words, and ushered me out the door. "We'll talk when you come out," he offered. Like a deer in headlights I froze. He was not coming in to join me. Awkwardly, I entered the store and embraced my fate, reminding myself that this is why I had spent four years in college.

After the ordeal I emerged from the store, tail between my legs. "Did you get the sale?" he asked.

"No," I mumbled.

"Did you learn anything?" Then it hit me. This was not about making sales, it was about the motivation to learn. I had been paying little attention to his first two presentations, thinking it would be a least a week before I would have to make my own (or so I thought). But now he had my attention. So, when he said, "I'll make the next two calls, then it's your turn again," I watched every move he made, peppering him with questions between stores. I was fulfilling an old Chinese proverb: "When the student is ready, the teacher appears."

Beginning with that experience I began to learn what constituted effective training. After six months in the field, Procter sent us to sales training school in Cincinnati because only then did we have enough experience "in the trenches" to appreciate the education we would receive. We had enough experience to know that we needed help and where we needed it most. And we were highly motivated to get it!

Training small group leaders is not much different, at least as far as training process is concerned. Modeling, practice, and interaction between teacher and learner are all essential components. When Jesus sent out the Twelve in Luke 9 or the Seventy in Luke 10, he had modeled the ministry and was now giving them firsthand experience. Afterward, they debriefed. He incorporated teaching, demonstration, experience, and discussion. His "classroom" was a place to share knowledge being learned in ministry settings and to demonstrate and practice skills together. It was a place for teaching truth. And the laboratory for leadership training was each new ministry situation. Our approach should be no different. Here are seven guidelines to consider when training leaders, particularly in the classroom.

### Address Real and Immediate Needs

Training actually becomes exciting when small group leaders acquire skills they can soon apply to their own small groups. Don't bother training leaders in skills that they "may need someday." Explain why the skills you are presenting will help them now. Stay in touch with current leadership obstacles so that your training meets your leaders' needs.

### Support with Scripture

Training events will appear too much like workplace training unless we feed and inspire leaders with truth from God's Word. Most small group skills are relational, and Scripture offers valuable advice about how to develop relationships, handle conflict, shepherd people, build spiritual disciplines into people, and lead with character.

### Train through Experiences

Experiential training is the most memorable and enjoyable. As people practice skills together and learn from one another, their confidence grows and their friendships deepen. In experiential learning, individuals do more than receive information; they develop a community of learning. For example, when you train people to lead prayer in a small group, be sure to have them actually lead a prayer time. Praying together not only gives firsthand experience with prayer, it also builds a stronger sense of community among leaders.

### Inspire and Motivate

Training should never be boring. Cast vision and tell stories. Remind people of why they are doing what they are doing and how important it is in the kingdom. Allow leaders to share success stories. Affirm them for the hard work that they do. Use creative materials, decorations, and activities so the environment is full of joy and excitement.

### Provide Tools and Resources

Leaders appreciate a new skill. But they enjoy it even more when they receive a tool or resource that helps them apply this skill in one of their next small group meetings. Pepper your training with group openers, teaching ideas, creative exercises, retreat ideas, prayer ideas, and other handouts that leaders can use in their own groups. If you keep these resources simple and user-friendly, leaders will eagerly attend your next training event.

### Keep It Focused

Never try to train more than two skills in a session. It's better to do brief, focused, practical, exciting training than to overwhelm leaders with twelve different skills. Training sessions of twenty to forty minutes are optimal. Once in awhile you will want to plan an official training morning or training day at church. But for ongoing training, it's best to provide short sessions that don't eat up your leader's time. Remember that they've already committed to leading a group and shepherding people.

### Don't Overtrain

We have tried to follow a principle Carl George has taught us—the more supervision you provide a leader, the less initial training they will require. If you plan on allowing them to lead alone without any supervision, then you must train them extensively before ever giving them a small group to work with. We have chosen to provide a moderate amount of initial training and then to supervise people throughout a lifetime of ministry. We call this supervision "coaching"—a role described in detail in the next chapter.

## Training Audience

When you train leaders, you cannot assume each one is starting on the front end of the learning curve. Some arrive at your church from other churches or ministries while others are novices. Priscilla and Aquila were novices when Paul met them as tentmakers, but Timothy had been taught by his mother and grandmother and was highly recommended by those in his church.

So it is in your setting. You will find that leaders fall into three categories—new, intermediate, and seasoned—and each has to be trained differently. Here are some suggestions for training each of these groups.

## New Leaders

We love new leaders. Most barely believe they can lead even when you know they are qualified. These reluctant leaders, whom we described earlier, must be given encouragement, the freedom to fail, and the skills to begin the small-group leadership adventure. When working with new leaders, give emphasis to the following areas:

- the role of leader-shepherd
- inviting people to the group
- leading a discussion
- guiding a prayer time
- promoting safety
- building a team
- casting a vision
- forming a covenant

These group fundamentals will help new leaders gain confidence. We recommend that many of the above skills be demonstrated in a group setting, in a "real" group or in a training class. New leaders are "show me" people, so keep the lectures brief and to the point. For example, here's a brief look at how to train leaders to ask questions that promote discussion. (See chart on next page.)

This kind of brief exercise will help new leaders gain confidence while they learn—and it can be done in a safe setting. "New" leaders may be seasoned Christians or even experienced people at work. But they are novices when leading a small group where the focus is authentic community. They will likely be nervous. Simple, brief exercises with encouraging feedback will get them off on the right foot.

## Intermediate Leaders

When leaders have progressed beyond the basics of their small group leadership experience or have been in another leadership setting that requires team or group skills, they are probably ready for some advanced skill training. These leaders understand the basics but have not

| **Setup** |
| --- |
| Form circles of five to six people |
| Choose a leader for each group |
| **Teach** |
| "The art of asking questions." Good questions are: |
| • open-ended rather than closed |
| • questions that invite opinion and experience |
| **Demonstrate** |
| Choose someone from the audience, interview them for five minutes asking open-ended questions. At the end, ask a closed-ended question so that the others can see how short the answer is. Closed-ended questions do not generate discussions; they seek answers or facts. Here are some examples: |
| *Open* |
| • How did you first find out about this church? |
| • What kind of work do you enjoy doing? Tell us more about it. |
| • What is the most rewarding aspect of being a father? |
| • Tell us about your high school experience. Describe what comes to mind as you think of it. |
| *Closed* |
| • How long does it take you to drive to church? |
| • What did you have for lunch? |
| **Practice** |
| Assign the leader at each table/group an open-ended question to ask someone. Ask the others at the table to respond only by asking more questions or seeking to understand the person who is talking. Encourage the use of "tell me more" and "it seems like" and "what I understand you are saying is," because these statements encourage more discussion. Remember, this will feel a little awkward, but it will make the point and help people not only to ask questions but to listen carefully. |
| **Feedback** |
| After three to five minutes of discussion, ask members at the table to debrief what they observed. How did the leader do? How did the members feel? What could be done differently? |
| Repeat two to three times with different questions and a different person assigned as the group leader each time. Have some fun. |
| At the end of the session, assign a spokesperson from each group to describe any key learning points or questions for the entire class. (Remember, it is ideal to practice this in a "real" small group using open-ended questions from a Bible passage. Later, after the meeting, debrief with your new leader-in-training, explaining why you asked certain questions.) |

yet mastered the art of leading small groups. Here are some areas of training you'll want to consider:

- intentional shepherding
- conflict resolution
- working with challenging members
- truth telling
- birthing a group
- developing an apprentice
- Bible study skills
- spiritual formation practices

Most of your work with these leaders will be done in huddles of four to six where they can share experiences and solve problems. Also, you'll spend some time providing advanced skill classes and some one-on-one mentoring. Gary Franklin of Fellowship Bible Church of Roswell, Georgia, has used the huddle effectively to train new and existing leaders. The coach and small group leaders meet together for training as a huddle. In this way, their coaches can understand what their leaders need and can build a leadership community while learning together. It also forges relationships between leaders that are essential to long-term leadership development and support. We'll talk more about this support, especially the role of coaches, in the next chapter.

### Seasoned Leaders

Once you have an experienced leader, your work becomes increasingly focused on advanced leadership skills and experiences instead of basic group dynamics. Moreover, experienced leaders are ready to help other leaders, either as assistant trainers or, in some cases, as coaches of other leaders. Less "training" and more "development" is required. Here are some of the areas to consider, though at this level, your focus will depend largely on the needs and progress of individual leaders.

- leading others through change
- coaching leaders toward growth
- leading serving projects and teams
- communication and teaching skills
- pastoral care in crisis situations
- group evangelism
- leading communion

We have discovered that the more leaders mature in their skills and character, the more essential it is to gather them together with other seasoned leaders for focused experiences. Retreats, leadership huddles, and exposure to veteran church leaders gives them the opportunity to ask questions and be challenged at new levels. Both of us have led groups of seasoned leaders for the purpose of expanding their horizons, enlarging their responsibilities, and building their character.

One of the great tragedies of church life is allowing a leader to plateau. If seasoned leaders are not challenged at new levels and if you fail to expose them to more substantive leadership experiences and relationships, you will lose them—to the workplace, the local community, and the sports world. This is not to say we should not lead in these areas. What we are saying is that the church needs to provide a playing field for our best and most gifted leaders, because if we do not, others will. Then the kingdom suffers.

As you design your training and development strategy for leaders, consider the methods and skills for new, intermediate, and seasoned leaders. If you are not sure what to do next, ask them. Most emerging leaders have a sense of what will take them to the next level. Then find the best people in your church to invest in these people because the small group ministry is only as effective as the quality and maturity of its leaders. Training them properly is essential. But supporting them for a lifetime of ministry is also imperative.

Great athletes need support in the form of people (coaches, family, and friends) and experiences (special camps, practices, films, and time with other experienced athletes) to maintain their competitive edge. Should not the church do at least as much for the people charged with the spiritual development of God's people—small group shepherds? So, as we move ahead, let's consider what leaders need in order to run the race to the finish with integrity and skill.

# 10

# Coaching and Supporting Leaders

*My life coach will see promise where others see a drearily blank slate. My life coach will invest in me as if I'm a hot new stock. My life coach will drill into my unrealized potential and extract a pot of gold.... I'd be a contender if I had a coach. Wouldn't you? Who wouldn't be a thousand times better, in everything from toothbrushing to planning out a life, if they had a coach to show them how it should be done, how much better it could be done, how much there is to win when it's done right?*

MARY SCHMICH, CHICAGO TRIBUNE

The best resource you can give a small group leader is a person. Soon after I (Bill) became small group pastor in another church, I began interviewing leaders. Almost everyone told me, "I feel like an island. Unless I call the church staff, no one contacts me." This church was not aware of Carl George's span of care principle (discussed in chapter 3) that everyone is cared for, but no one should care for more than ten. This principle applies to leaders of small groups as well as to coaches who shepherd small group leaders.

In the church where leaders felt isolated, I had as many as forty-five small group leaders under my care. Among that group I found myself giving attention to two types of people: the ones I really liked and the ones who complained the most. Everyone in the middle was ignored. That's because my span of care was violated. Though we at Willow Creek find that leaders can care for ten small group members, we limit a coach's span of care to five small group leaders.

## The Coach's Span of Care

This smaller span of care makes sense when you understand the coach's role, ministry setting, place within the church structure, and relationship to individual leaders. To support leaders and coaches for a lifetime of ministry, your church will need to pray, create events, and set up support systems.

### The Coach's Role

Small group leaders depend on their coaches for shepherding, support, prayer, new ideas, and, sometimes, a kind voice on the phone. The chart below outlines a coach's ministry description.

**The Role of the Coach**

|  | Huddle | Visiting the Group | One-on-One |
|---|---|---|---|
| **Leadership Development**<br>• vision casting<br>• skills<br>• apprentices | *Lead* | *Affirm* | *Care* |
| **Pastoral Care**<br>• spiritual<br>• relational<br>• personal | and | and | and |
| **Ministry Support and Expansion**<br>• prayer<br>• affirmation<br>• resources | *Model* | *Observe* | *Develop* |

The left column describes the coach's role. We expect coaches to help develop leaders by keeping them equipped, helping them grow, and looking for potential leaders within each group. Coaches remember that every leader is a person; they provide care for leaders by showing love for who they are, not simply for what they do. Coaches support each leader's ministry by connecting them to necessary resources, such as curriculum, training, or prayer support. (For a full explanation of a coach's role, responsibilities, and ministry methods, you can request the *Willow Creek Coaches Handbook* available from the Willow Creek Association.)

## The Coach's Ministry Setting

The top row of the above chart describes the three primary settings—huddle meeting, group visit, one-on-one—in which a coach interacts with leaders.

### Huddle Meetings

Coaches gather some or all their small group leaders for huddle meetings. During these meetings, which usually last sixty to ninety minutes, coaches lead and model leadership. They guide leaders toward more effective ministry, build community, share ideas, gather information about the groups, and envision the leaders.

### Group Visits

Coaches visit small group meetings to make verbal affirmations and mental observations. They make affirmations such as "It's great to be with you and see all of you together encouraging one another toward growth in Christ." They remind group members how fortunate they are to have a shepherd.

When coaches make such visits, we encourage them to organize their mental observations according to the LEAD (Lead, Environment, Apprentice, Dynamic) acrostic. First, the coach affirms and observes the *leader*. Coaches check out whether leaders prepare and run meetings effectively, need resources, and show love for their members. Basically, the coach looks for ways to serve and support leaders.

Second, the coach mentally evaluates whether the *environment* is conducive to life change. Is the meeting space appropriate? Is the open chair being used or discussed in the group? Does this feel like a safe group where people can express their feelings and opinions without being judged critically or ignored?

Third, the coach makes sure that each leader has an *apprentice* and that the apprentice is participating. Coaches help leaders find ways to develop apprentices and assess their readiness to lead a group.

Finally, the coach takes a read on the group *dynamic* by looking at how members treat each other and handle conflict. The coach notices whether members simply answer questions or actually engage in discussions where truth meets life.

## One-on-One Meetings

Coaches spend much of their time in one-on-one meetings with each leader. They use this time to care for small group leaders' needs and develop them toward the next step in spiritual maturity. We are interested in them as people, not just as leaders. Coaches talk with leaders about their family lives, work relationships, and personal goals as well as their difficulties as followers of Christ. Using the Five Gs shepherding plan helps coaches and leaders mutually assess and discern the next steps for each other's growth and for deepening their relationships.

## Building a Coaching Structure

Understanding a coach's role and function is easier than integrating these key leaders into church life and structure. "Building a coaching structure is one of the biggest challenges of small group ministry," says Don Neff, associate pastor of The Worship Center in Lancaster, Pennsylvania.

The Worship Center has weekend attendance of about 2,650, with sixty section leaders (coaches) and 152 small groups. About 75 percent of the congregation is in small groups, based on a cell model designed by Korean minister Dr. David Cho. In 1984, The Worship Center's senior pastor and some lay leaders went to Korea to attend a church growth seminar about growing a church through small groups, as Dr. Cho did.

"We never made this radical shift," Neff said. "We built groups underground, and God was causing some sort of success." Like the Korean cell model, The Worship Center's groups are geographically based. The church tried to incorporate Dr. Cho's basic principles: pray over your geographic area, find a need and fill it, and raise up leaders to multiply groups.

"We took the existing groups, and we shared the vision," Neff said. "Early on, people got the vision and saw the necessity. Ministry growth was slow and sure—a natural process with most groups birthing from older groups. Most groups were birthed out of our living room, so the coaches came out of that."

Some of the church's sixty coaches, called section leaders, serve as couples, so there are actually thirty-nine coaching "units." Each coach or coaching couple oversees three to six group leaders—providing shepherding, helping groups, and acting as a point of contact for pastoral care from the church.

Getting people to coach requires casting a vision. "It's a strategic role," Neff says. "We call them and say, 'We've seen what you've been doing as a leader, and we think you could do this successfully.' We show them the way, help them to grow personally in their walk with God."

Neff typically gives his coaches two other groups to coach while they continue to lead their own group for a while. "It's an easier transition, and they can grow into it," he says. "Good leaders can't always be good coaches. Going slow reveals that." Coaches, or section leaders, go through a one-time, six-hour training and have monthly meetings with their small group leaders. District leaders (similar to Willow's division leaders) are part-time staff who care for section leaders.

When five district leaders attended the Willow Creek Association's Small Groups Conference, Neff says they "came back *changed*, really impacted. We had run out of models to follow. We really liked what Dr. Cho taught, but some of the cultural things didn't translate. That conference helped us go to the next level."

## The Coach's Relationship to the Leader

Coaches are primarily lovers of leaders. Love is the overriding Christian virtue, and it must be expressed between leaders. A leader who is loved is a leader who will serve well for a long time. A leader who is loved is a leader who will respond to correction or training. A leader who is loved is a leader who can be given more responsibility, because he or she will receive it appropriately. So, much of coaching is simply loving.

People often ask us, "How do you get your leaders to come to so many events? You want them to lead a small group and attend church services—plus participate in training events or retreats. How do you get them there?" We love them there. It's the only authentic way to do it. When a leader understands that you care more about them than you do about their "job," then a lot can happen to further Christ's cause.

Sometimes loving means asking someone to step out of leadership. These are not happy moments, but they can be fruitful ones. Whether it is because of moral failure or performance issues, removing a leader is a painful process. It must be done, however, for the health of the body. Remember, leaders have been given spiritual authority to shepherd others toward growth. If we allow problem leaders to remain in positions of leadership, we are allowing them to inflict damage on Christ's body. We handle this process much as we handle conflicts within small groups (as described in chapter 6).

A coach should never act alone in removing someone from leadership. Staff and/or elders must be involved. Together, with grace, love, and the promise of restoration and support, a leader can be removed and discipled toward a future ministry role. Be direct, clear, and gracious as you seek closure. If, over time, a leader receives the correction well and learns from mistakes, then you have won a brother or sister.

## Supporting Leaders for a Lifetime of Ministry

Leaders are the key to building a church of small groups. They will guide groups toward authentic relationships, help people engage with transforming truth, promote healthy conflict resolution among members, and shepherd people toward mutual care and growth. Without leaders, the ministry becomes fractured and unfocused. Leaders embrace the values and vision of your church; they deliver a common consistent message to the congregation.

Support leaders in every way you can so they remain effective for a long time. We have already explained that the best way to support a leader is with a person, a coach. But we can also support their ministries through prayer, events, and systems.

### Support through Prayer

John 17 tells how Jesus asked the Father to protect his future leaders "from the evil one." Jesus understood that community building is a spiritual battle. Building a church of small groups engages the enemy on the front line of kingdom expansion and maturity. So Jesus prayed for his leaders, and we must do the same. At Willow Creek, coaches and staff members pray for leaders, and our prayer team devotes time and energy to specific praying for our church leaders. We believe this intercessory prayer for leaders at all levels has strengthened and protected them. Countless spiritual battles have probably been won without any of us really knowing it. Prayer supports, protects, and paves the way for future ministries. It puts leaders close to God's heart, so they understand his purposes and follow in submission and confidence.

When I (Bill) was leading our couples ministry at Willow Creek, one coach experienced significant growth in his division. The coaching huddle had grown from two small groups to eight, which is beyond the normal size. Each group had an apprentice leader, and the coach was developing an apprentice coach. I pulled him aside one day at church and asked, "What is your strategy for raising up all of these leaders? This process takes much longer for most other coaches than it seems to take for you."

His response was simple and direct. "Prayer," he said. "I pray that God will give me the spiritual eyes to see emerging leaders or people with potential to lead. Then I approach them and begin to work with them."

"Yes," I responded, "but what is your *strategy*?" At this point he must have thought I was a spiritual dwarf, because a second time he said to me, "Prayer—that's my strategy." It was not one of my best leadership moments, but it certainly was one of his. He understood it. Leadership development is a spiritual battle, and this man had understood how to fight it. He was praying for new leaders and he was praying for his existing leaders. He knew there could be no numerical growth and no spiritual growth in the lives of his people without persistent prayer.

## Support through Events

Throughout the year, you'll need to gather leaders for mutual encouragement, support, teaching, feeding, and envisioning. At Willow Creek, we vary the numbers and kinds of leadership support events, because each ministry season or phase requires a different focus. We have used several kinds of events to support leaders.

### Annual Small Group Leaders Retreat

This is a "can't miss" event at Willow Creek. Because we are now a church of small groups, the entire leadership structure of the church is present—staff, coaches, small group leaders, elders, board members. We design this retreat primarily to inspire everyone and clarify the vision for the coming ministry season. It is a combination pep rally, worship celebration, teaching opportunity, and community-building event.

We spend about 80 percent of our time celebrating, encouraging leaders, teaching them from the Scriptures, and allowing them to interact with one another for mutual edification and idea sharing. This is the "feeding" portion of the retreat. To *feed* our leaders then gives us the right to *lead* them toward common ministry objectives. A leadership challenge, often given by Bill Hybels or Russ Robinson, allows all of us to orient our ministry focus in a common direction. After all, we are building a church—not simply leading a coalition of fragmented small groups, each with its own agenda.

We have often held this retreat off campus, which is just plain fun because it allows people to disconnect from the church environment and from family and work demands. The downside, however, is that it costs more to rent a retreat facility or ask leaders to provide childcare while they're away for a day or two.

Recently we have held the annual retreat on campus at Willow Creek, which costs less, uses familiar facilities and equipment, and is more accessible to more leaders. The disadvantage of on-campus retreats is that leaders are more likely to be drawn back home by family distractions and thus miss some sessions. Therefore, it becomes our responsibility to provide a retreat with such great content and experiential learning that leaders will not want to miss it.

## Leadership Community

Many churches see the benefit of regular leadership gatherings, often on a monthly or quarterly basis. Sometimes Leadership Community meetings include time for coaches to huddle with their small group leaders. We offer training opportunities throughout the year, but during Leadership Community we focus on vision, ministry direction, mutual edification, and idea sharing.

Park Community Church makes sure its Leadership Community relates to the church's urban context. Located in the heart of Chicago, Park Community is mainly a congregation of young urban professionals who, apart from church, feel somewhat isolated. "The city is such a crazy place," says Kevin Phillips, small groups director. "People feel disconnected, whether they are single or married. But we are first and foremost a city church. People in the city are clamoring for community. Some are singles, in their first job, separated from their family. They are relationally hungry. And even the urban family doesn't always have the opportunities to connect with others on a deeper level."

Park has about sixty-five small groups, which connect an estimated five hundred people into groups. When we interviewed Phillips, all the groups were studying the same curriculum, a Bible study of Galatians written and published by the church. "We put together some material with questions and group exercises, and we're going through it together as a church," Phillips says. "We found that people sometimes struggled with what to study. This gave them an option, and all of them liked it. The groups have material that they trust."

Phillips explains that monthly leadership training and huddles help "grow the quality of the ministry." These meetings include prayer, worship, and training on topics such as truth-telling and encouragement.

## Coaches' Gatherings

From time to time we find it helpful to gather our coaches. Sometimes we gather them for an annual retreat to emphasize the importance of their work as shepherds of leaders. Willow Creek is so large that many coaches' gatherings take place at the subministry level of ministries to men, women, children, and so on. Coaches come together for a light meal or snack and meet with other staff and ministry leaders for skill training, prayer, resource sharing, and problem solving.

## Celebration Events

As we became a church of small groups, we found it helpful to pause at the end of each ministry season and celebrate God's work through small groups. These celebration events include storytelling, worship, and expressions of gratitude. We used to have these events for the whole church—which is probably preferable—but we have grown so large that most of them now take place by ministry. Either way, it's valuable to celebrate God's work and validate the influence of small group ministry in church life.

## Special Conferences

Sometimes your leaders need to hear the vision of someone outside your church, whether you invite a guest speaker to your retreat or take your leaders to a place that shares your vision and values. The second option worked well for Faith Lutheran Church in Troy, Michigan.

During the church's first thirty-five years, several leaders tried to start small groups. Each time, up to ten groups would begin, but within a year they would dissolve. Faith Lutheran had just two small groups when Tim Kade became associate pastor in 1999. "A few people would say that we ought to have groups, and they'd get people together and tell them, 'Start a group.' But we didn't know how to equip or resource people," Kade says.

"Some folks would start fellowship groups, while others would go the opposite extreme and have a serious, seminary-class type Bible study. Leaders got no help or contact until six months to a year later, when a staff person would call to see how the group was doing—and be surprised to learn that it was no longer meeting," he adds.

So Kade set up a training program, which taught people how to lead a group. "What I've done differently is believe in people," he said. "I see in them what God has the potential to do through them, even before they see it."

By October 1999, Faith Lutheran had launched seventeen new groups. Kade says attending our Small Groups Conference the following year was a huge turning point. He had hoped to take a few leaders, but wasn't sure whether volunteer leaders would take three days off work to learn about small groups. "I would have been excited if five people from our church came," he said. But instead, God stirred the hearts of twenty-one people to attend the conference together. These people represented various ministries, and, at the conference, this core group realized that "the Lord was laying on us the desire to see the dream of God's community become a reality at our church."

By the end of 2000, Faith Church had forty adult and eight youth small groups. The children's ministry, called Kid's Connection, had twenty-five groups. With a weekend attendance of about 2,400, Kade says, "a ton of people still aren't connected. But most of our groups are full, and we've got thirty-five people on a waiting list."

The conference helped Faith Lutheran catch the vision. So did Kade's policy of encouraging people to just "try" leading for a year. "I tell them, 'What would it be like to have a church like this? Wouldn't it be exciting?' I use the analogy of a rubber band and ask them, 'Will you allow God to stretch you?' A rubber band is only useful when it's stretched," Kade remarks.

To get more people interested in small groups and leadership, this church has hosted a small group fair and a fall festival, where people could sign up for groups. Kade is also setting up a coaching structure.

While his vision casting and training has influenced the growth, Kade says, "The catalyst for all of the excitement goes back to the Small Groups Conference. The vision . . .was not only inspiring, but it equipped us with the skills to go back and put into practice the things we learned." Don't neglect the power of events to restore vision and hope for leaders!

## Support through Systems

As your small group ministry grows and multiplies, you will need systems to monitor its growth and allocate staff and resources. This process is relatively simple when you have only five to ten small groups.

Once you have thirty or more groups, however, you will become acutely aware of the need for a basic database to track leaders, groups, coaches, and the flow of people in and out of groups. As the small group ministry has evolved at Willow Creek, we have developed tools to support the ministry at each phase.

Early on we required a small group report after every meeting. This served us well for a season because it was a new ministry, and we wanted to be well apprised of each group's experience. Soon this became a monthly report and, later, a quarterly ministry profile. *Leading Life-Changing Small Groups* includes a sample report from those early days.

You will also need a communications system to inform leaders and coaches of ministry opportunities and updates. We have used a newsletter, an insert in our weekly bulletin, and a quarterly tape. Now we are experimenting with other technology-based communications systems. The important thing is to inform your people without overwhelming them. Keep your communications brief, essential, and creative.

Effectively deploying small group leaders to build a church of groups is serious business, requiring great effort and prayer. But rest assured that honoring the priesthood of believers by equipping them for ministry is well worth the investment. Knowing how to identify, recruit, coach, and support leaders will make all the difference in the world. You will release an army of committed shepherds who understand what they are supposed to do, are inspired to do it, believe God has called them to ministry, and feel equipped and supported by you.

# LEADING A CHURCH OF SMALL GROUPS

Part 4

**G**reg Hawkins is Willow Creek Community Church's executive pastor. A Stanford MBA, he left a fast-track career at the international consulting firm McKenzie and Company to become a Willow Creek intern during the start-up of our transition to becoming a church of small groups. Since Greg is a systems genius, his fingerprints are still evident on our small groups ministry.

Greg's fingerprints are always on display, because he is a tall Texan who cannot speak without exuberantly moving his hands. Whenever he describes his passion—whether for cooking, painting, theology, science, his family, or the church and its leaders—we feel like we're watching an improvisational floor show. Sit too close, and you risk injury from demonstrative explanation.

Imagine Greg's two hands spread far apart, one above the other, their long fingers stretching a rubber band to its breaking point. We first saw this image come to life when he described the gap between vision (the upper hand) and reality (the lower hand). The rubber band stretched between his large hands represented the tension such a gap creates. The larger the gap, the greater the tension.

Building a church of small groups is a tension-filled venture. On the one hand, it requires mind-boggling vision. God imagines and expects churches will be filled with relationships of oneness, just like his. He sees us as capable of, even designed for, such oneness, and he knows the benefits we get every time we invest in community. He anticipates his church will weave oneness-level texture into its life. God assumes leaders will pay attention to people's needs, design appropriate spans of care, and connect sin-stained people into caring, life-transforming friendships via little communities.

On the other hand there is reality. All that vision is useless unless it is translated into the life of one average group of people, then diffused so the whole church starts to experience life in little communities. Unless and until there is a network of small groups—where relationships are authentic, truth touches life, conflict is resolved, and shepherding happens—the gap between vision and reality will produce tension. Pressure will increase unless you support this new network with effective leadership.

Most of us dislike tension and avoid it if we can. Yet the gap between God's vision and our reality demands attention. Church leaders have never been able to avoid such organizational pressures. Old Testament kings, God's shepherds of the day, were called to account for their sheep, and early church apostles had to reorganize to meet needs. The Bible gives countless examples of how people entrusted to lead either dealt with the vision/reality tension or failed, to their detriment.

Gifted leaders recognize, of course, that tension creates opportunities to help people. Point out a gap to most leaders, and they energetically respond with solutions. They are not content with status quo. Once the vision is clear, they start working on the gap between vision and reality.

This section explains how to narrow the gap. It helps you envision the changes your church must make if you want to express community through small groups. Unless you deal with these issues, your transition to small groups will deteriorate into just another church program. We know how hard it is to maintain a clear vision of creating communities that offer the oneness Christ expects, the unity he prayed for while facing death. We began our transition in 1992, and we are still trying to move parts of our vision to reality. But we can offer a blueprint of necessary changes that will help mature your church body on a small groups skeleton.

First, your church must recognize and act on five key decisions during your transition (chapter 11). Some decisions will result in minor changes, while others will require rebuilding parts of your organizational foundation. If you ignore any of these decisions, your rubber band will snap.

Second, you must choose a strategy for building a church of small groups (chapter 12). You probably already know of several ministry models for growing groups, such as cell or metachurch strategies. We will focus on the six core principles necessary to any change strategy, no matter which model you choose for building small groups.

Finally, we will look at how your church can phase in a small groups infrastructure (chapter 13). Some churches are just starting to see the value of small group life but haven't embraced the larger vision of oneness or clarified how small groups work. Others have started their journey but need better transition plans. We will explain the predictable phases most churches experience before they are ready to "go public" with small groups. Our stories show that since small groups involve people and churches, the real-life process is not nearly as linear as we'd sometimes like! But the general principles we offer will help you move your congregation to become a church of small groups.

# 11

# Make Decisions

*Few leaders ever encounter times of great moral crisis on a soci-
etal level. But they are called upon every day to face hard real-
ities, to cut through conflicting currents and ambiguities and to
stake out clear positions.*

NOEL TICHY, THE LEADERSHIP ENGINE

Willow Creek Community Church has made its share of mistakes on the
way to becoming a church of small groups. Well, let's be real: *we* (Russ
and Bill) have made many mistakes—none of them fatal—on this journey. You can learn from our errors.

Fortunately, Willow Creek's senior leaders made wise decisions from
the start. Looking back, we can identify five key questions we asked in
order to become a church of small groups:

- Will we become a church of small groups?
- Who will be the point leader?
- What will be our long-range structure?
- How will we develop enough leaders?
- From where are we starting?

Each of these questions became forks in the road to determining our
future direction in ministry. Our leaders most often chose the right path.
Your church will face the same five forks. Each is easy to overlook; yet,
the decisions you make (or ignore) will have lasting effects.

## Become a Church of Small Groups

Deciding to shift our small group approach was hard because our group-
based discipleship program was thriving *as originally intended*. Staff and

volunteers had invested their minds, hearts, and souls in it. The former small group ministry got me (Russ) and my wife, Lynn, into our first little community at church; the group we led bore wonderful fruit. Besides our discipleship groups, the church had departments devoted to women, singles, evangelism, and more. Yet, too many people lacked a sense of ministry identity. There was no way to build enduring relationships, little chance for everyone to experience biblical community.

We faced our first fork. Willow could remain a church *with* small groups. This meant increased attendance at outstanding services and ministries for select needs. For more serious discipling, people could join a small group, complete the two-year *Walking with God* curriculum, then lead their own group. The costs were fixed and we knew the consequences.

Or Willow could build a church *of* small groups—a promising future with substantial but unknown cost. At minimum, senior leaders knew it would require radical restructuring at every level. To their credit, Willow's leaders "got it." Once they saw the decision, they made it.

First Presbyterian Church of Bethlehem, Pennsylvania, chose to change—and learned that transition takes time. "First Pres" became a church *with* groups in the 1960s, when its current membership process began. Prospective members enter an eight-week Inquirers' Group to study the church's five key values, "the TGs": touched by grace, trained in groups, tuned to gifts, tested with grief, tempered for goodness. About 90 percent of interested inquirers continue for one year, with their leaders, in Koinonia groups. A quarter of the church's 3,300 members remains in small groups; half move on to ministry teams; some do both.

But Pastor Gareth Icenogle, who taught at Fuller Theological Seminary and wrote *Biblical Foundations of Small Group Ministry*, says, "*Everything* we do has got to be about developing disciples. Our mission statement is 'turning seekers of God into servants of Jesus.'" He estimates his congregation is halfway toward becoming a church *of* groups.

In 1993 First Pres built an award-winning building and reorganized the children's ministry into small groups. Divided into six "neighborhoods," each formed by soundproof dividers into four-room clusters, the new building provides for both small- and large-group time. "We call it architectural koinonia. People say it feels like a family," Icenogle says. "Our task groups, such as ushers, are beginning to understand the whole idea and language of 'team.' We want these groups to include prayer, Bible study, and mutual support."

First Pres recently began using Greg Ogden's triad method to develop leaders (described in the book *Discipleship Essentials*). One mentor shepherds two disciples, who also encourage and train each other. "We wanted something more fluid than a one-on-one hierarchy," Icenogle points out.

Willow and First Pres clearly decided to become churches *of* groups. We have seen, in far too many churches, the consequences of ignoring this decision. In fact, when we are in a room teaching about why churches must face this decision, we have seen church leaders become ill—because they suddenly see the chaos they've spawned by rushing ahead without a congregational commitment to become a church of groups.

Too often, a pastor or key layperson catches the small group vision, which spreads through conversations, meetings, and committees. Everyone thinks "more community" sounds great, and leaders make changes. But no one defines the outcome or clarifies the consequences.

Senior pastors who neglect this fork will realize, too late, that to model small group life as normative, they need to change their schedules. They will be baffled by how the new small group network complicates their ability to preach to a singular, gathered audience. As new little communities deepen vulnerability, inevitable relational conflicts will explode emotional shrapnel, hitting the senior pastor who skipped past the hard choice: church *with* or church *of*? Asked to transition their ministries into small groups, volunteers will cry, "Bait and switch!" Vague "church of" moves can easily result in relational wounds, disillusioned staff, and volunteer withdrawals.

Decide. Then communicate regularly and pointedly what you are, without apology. We prefer the "church of groups" choice, but definitively choosing "church with" is far better than confusion.

## Use Centralized Point Leadership

As Windy City residents learned during the Chicago Bulls' glory years, even with a star like Michael Jordan, the team needs a point guard—someone to bring the basketball down the court and call the plays. This on-court commander is the difference between winning and losing. Likewise, we want a "point leader" for every Willow ministry. Deciding to choose a small groups point leader is the second fork on the road to becoming a church of small groups.

We have seen the distress and discord that result when churches ignore this decision. Some add the small group responsibility to the job description of the person least able to protest, such as the new youth pastor or Christian education director. Already overloaded, these people lack the preparation or passion to change the church infrastructure. Other churches try to divide and conquer, saying, "We'll all do some." This approach avoids the pain of changing the staff line-up, but avoided confrontation yields lousy organizational design and fragmented results. Still other congregations see small groups as a field of dreams—"If we build it, they will come"—but don't give *anyone* the responsibility to close the gap between vision and reality. Meanwhile, the pioneers who risked trying small group life watch it all fall apart, for lack of a point leader to champion the mission.

Willow Creek has had a small groups point leader since 1992, because, as Bill Hybels puts it, "Somebody has to sleep on the cot." Jim Dethmer started the effort; Jon Wallace came from Azusa Pacific University to lead it for eighteen months; then Willow Creek hired me (Russ). I went from being a lawyer who led one small group to being a minister in charge of a ministry to eight thousand small group members.

I (Bill) remember the uneasy day we heard that our new boss had little proven small group experience. But he had recognized leadership gifts, and we helped him acquire ministry expertise. We have seen the wisdom of point leadership because, by teaming the right people under a leader who championed the mission, we have realized the dream of becoming a church of small groups.

Someone must play point leader. If you cannot afford to hire such a person, then choose a key layperson willing to play an unpaid staff role. Look for someone with these traits: spiritual gifts of leadership and administration, strategic thinking, proven history in building organizations, and spiritual life worth imitating.

Clearly define the point leader's role. We look at the Willow Creek Director of Small Groups as a "first among equals," who envisions the church and its leaders to build community, strategizes the next steps, plans whole-church events and communications, monitors progress, and provides accountability. While making on-court plays to build a group-based church, the point leader needs support from the whole team, but especially from the senior pastor.

"Leadership sets the tone for the organization," says John Wiseman. As small group pastor at First Alliance in Calgary, Alberta, he understands the importance of point leadership and the senior pastor's role.

First Alliance became a church of small groups after its senior pastor of twenty-two years retired. "People looked to the new pastor, Terry Young, to take us to the next step," Wiseman says. Young cast a vision that distinguished a life group from a Bible study. He taught that all verses exhorting believers to minister to "one another" make up a biblical mandate for small groups. The church elders spent eight months studying Carl George's book *The Coming Church Revolution*. First Alliance began requiring small group participation for membership.

"This is a paradigm shift for a ninety-year-old congregation used to traditional Bible study groups. We have not pressured them. Rather, we have invited them to training. We chaplain them," Wiseman says, adding that Terry Young's clear vision is key. "He is passionate. On Sunday morning, he'll say, 'We need eight more leaders this week,' or he'll share how his faith was advanced in his own small group. People respond." Within two years, the number of small groups jumped from forty to 135; church attendance now averages 1,600 adults and 400 children.

## Design and Build a Long-Range Structure

Scripture admonishes us to "count the cost." Our parents gave us the common sense to look before we leap. "Begin with the end in mind," Steven Covey advises in *Seven Habits of Highly Effective People*. For congregations on the road to populating their entire church with little communities, the third fork is designing a structure to support such change.

Lynn and I (Russ) recently experienced proof that beginning with a good design is better than retooling a structure later. Our home burned down, and we spent hours with the architect we hired to design our new home. We also invited our architect and general contractor to meet with us together. The meeting went well until the contractor examined the final page of blueprints. "How tall is the side wall for your walkout basement?" he asked. The architect said it was eight feet, standard in the U.S. Midwest.

The contractor kept leafing through pages and making calculations. Finally he said, "You won't like this, but we should raise the foundation wall one foot. Once we put in the major support beam to span your oversize basement playroom, we'll have to drop the ceiling eighteen inches. The middle of the playroom ceiling will be just four inches above your head, Russ."

Here was the problem: raising the basement one foot affected every part of the house design. We had to lengthen staircases, which then protruded into rooms, which in turn meant we had to redraft, pay for more materials, and alter some favorite details. But it had to be done if we wanted the playroom to function well. Now that we are in the house, we're glad we faced the issue at the outset. Despite the interruption of a seemingly minor issue, our builder served us well by beginning with the end in mind.

Though Willow Creek chose to be a church of small groups and chose a small groups point leader, it missed the third fork. We made our transition without a complete blueprint, still using old programs and ministries—and we have paid the price of retooling. Clearly, we could not have anticipated every twist our path has taken, but had we planned more completely, we may have avoided many reorganizations, personnel shifts, and resulting turbulence.

Learn from our experience: pull together a group of people who love "org charts," so you can evaluate how small groups will affect your infrastructure. Think of your church leaders as architects and your point leader as the builder. *Design your structure as if everything you envision for your church came true.*

Ginghamsburg United Methodist in Tipp City, Ohio (near Dayton), understands that becoming a church of small groups requires more than simply adapting a "metachurch model." Ten years ago, the church committed to the metachurch structure of cell-group ministry, says Dan Glover, discipleship director for three years. When the church moved into a larger building, weekly attendance soared from 1,300 to 3,000 (where it remains) within eighteen months.

"The growth happened while we were still learning what 'meta' is. Our structure drifted away from intentional discipleship into administrative accountability," Glover says. Groups provided fellowship and a sense of connection to the church, but not much discipleship.

Ginghamsburg United Methodist now has 1,200 members and 310 groups—87 discipleship groups, including youth ministry and adult home groups; 25 support groups; and 198 task groups, such as ushers and sound support teams. "We want to look at meta as a discipling structure and fill it with relationships. Our goal for the next five to seven years is to transform our task groups into fully functioning cell groups that will grow mature followers while also accomplishing the task," Glover says.

Some groups still want to focus only on getting the job done. "As they wear out—dog-tired and drained from trying to do ministry without discipleship—they're willing to start talking with me," he goes on to say. Glover has revised his handbook for small group leaders, so home groups become places for spiritual growth, not just fellowship. "We tell leaders, 'We're not interested in what you can produce. We're interested in Christ being formed in you.'"

Glover is writing a team pastor (coach) handbook and rebuilding the coaching structure so that team pastors will be less likely to also serve in task groups. "Once team pastors are introduced to discipling, some dismiss themselves. Or, they dump their other jobs at church. They don't have time for both, now that we're asking them to go beyond keeping track of groups to actually pouring God's truth into leaders. It's a big shift from religious activity to building discipling relationships, and that's not easy."

As you design a structure for the church you envision, look at every part of your church. Plan how you'll transform existing boards and committees into little communities. How will you inject small groups into ministry to children, men, the hurting, missions, and other target groups? Pinpoint which staff and volunteers will be affected and whether some programs won't be needed anymore. Discuss how your current nomenclature will work in the new structure. Assume low-, mid-, and high-growth scenarios; each will present different challenges to your design.

Becoming a church of small groups changed how Willow Creek did evangelism. For years we simply asked this ministry to train believers to share their faith, rally those with evangelism gifts, and be a resource to seekers. We had to ask hard questions about how such a ministry could be rooted in a small group system. The answer was "seeker small groups," where a Christian leader and apprentice gather lost friends in a safe, community-based environment to explore their faith. After they commit their lives to Christ, those new Christians then meet with the leader (between seeker group meetings) for discipleship in their new-found faith. However, they still remain in their original seeker groups to encourage others in their search. Instead of a single department of relatively few loosely-connected Christians, we now have over a thousand people connected into community.

## Establish a Strategy for Developing Your Leadership

The fourth fork in the road is the ultimate reality check in building a church of small groups. Deploying community throughout your church will involve the most intensive leadership effort you can imagine. Unless you figure out how to identify, develop, and place enough leaders, your congregation will run out of steam before becoming a group-based church.

When my (Russ) wife taught elementary school, she loved instructing children in science, history, social studies, spelling, and art. Though Lynn did well with most arithmetic, she, like many people, had trouble with word problems. So she and I had fun working on them together. All our practice on word problems serves me now as I direct small group ministry, because building a church of small groups is like solving a word problem.

As described in Exodus 18, your church, like Moses, must ask: How many leaders does it take to build a structure in which everybody is cared for—but nobody cares for too many? Regardless of your design, you will find that you need a number of leaders equal to 25 or 30 percent of the number of people connected in groups. That high percentage includes those who are apprentices or rising apprentices, people who are intentionally being developed as emerging leaders. Thus, a group of ten will have a leader, an apprentice, and maybe one or two others the leader hopes to develop as future leaders.

If your church numbers 300 today, that means 75 leaders; if it is 500, it will take 125; if 1,000 people will be in groups, you will need over 300 prepared leaders. Yes, at Willow Creek that means we have had to identify almost 5,000 coaches, leaders, apprentices, and other volunteers—though we didn't need them all the first day of beginning our new infrastructure.

This fork in the road will force you to consider at least four issues.

*First, a church built on a small groups foundation will have to create a movement of volunteers like never before.* Your teaching will need to own and live out the priesthood of all believers as well as scriptural emphasis on both leadership and "follower-ship." Recruiting, placing, and supporting volunteers will define church health.

*Second, you need to invest in volunteer leaders.* You will have to design and deliver training, solve practical problems, reallocate budgets, and create tracking systems.

*Third, you will give away ministry to an increasing corps of lay ministers.* As people redefine their lives around ministry, they'll become tentmakers, blending their church and professional lives. Your pastoral staff will truly become equippers of laity.

*Last, there is good news: the ownership of the congregation's life will expand.* Raising funds will be less difficult, since many lay ministers see the difference their resources make. Staff hires will reflect excellence in the selection process as a result of a growing familiarity with actual personnel needs. Lay leaders will enter into ministry as a lifestyle choice. As average women and men get involved in church life, they will naturally share that life with friends and neighbors. The church will reflect the biblical picture of a multifaceted functional body of Christ.

Willow Creek's ushers and greeters provide a supreme example of such ownership. We had trouble retaining ushers and greeters until a team of staff and volunteer leaders began to dream of being an example to the rest of the body. Over time, they introduced change so dutiful service became noble service. They trained leaders to own the entire ministry; staff became bystanders. Several laypeople took early retirement to lead the cause of being Christ's hands and feet to guests who enter his house. They now include lost friends through their JHABO strategy—Just Hand A Bulletin Out. Many people have found salvation in Christ by starting as lost servants here. The dramatic change among our ushers and greeters is the kind you can expect when your church opts for radical inclusiveness of laity into leadership.

## Define Your Current Reality

You know what you want to be, who will lead the charge, how the ministry will look, and when you will need leaders. You have a preferred future in mind. But to get from here to there, you have to assess "here." The final fork is thoroughly evaluating your church's current status. The following diagnostic questions will help.

### From Where Have We Come?

Imagine a 128-year-old traditional church in rural Iowa where, for generations, the pastors provided all the leadership and pastoral care. Imagine a church with 2,000 people on its membership rosters, but less than half actually attending services and very few using their gifts or serving in any way.

Then imagine a new senior pastor with a new vision. Dean Hess knew his flock needed spiritual growth and pastoral care, but—given that four of the previous six pastors had burned out and no longer pastored anywhere—he knew he couldn't succeed alone. Yet, Zion Lutheran's mostly elderly congregation wanted the pastor—no one else—to teach adult Sunday School; they didn't want to discuss life application. The hundred homebound members expected regular home visits, preferably from the senior pastor.

Hess attended a Church Leadership Conference at Willow Creek. Twelve years ago he had read *Prepare Your Church for the Future,* by Carl George, and thought, "I want to pastor a church like that, a church of small groups." Six years ago he hired a couple fresh from seminary. Jonathan Swenson was director of youth and education; Jana was director of small group ministry—except the church didn't yet have any small groups.

"While Jana began new adult groups, I transitioned youth and children from a Sunday School model to small groups," Jonathan says. Hess and his associate had taught the seventh- and eighth-grade confirmation class, lecture style. "Now the kids are trained by lay volunteers, and they learn in small groups with other kids. When kids are confirmed, they name their small group leader as their biggest spiritual influence," Jonathan Swenson says.

Zion Lutheran is becoming a church of small groups, with the emphasis on becoming. The senior pastor's vision drove this process, but he has taken hits for this and for not doing all the pastoral care himself. The church now has sixty-five adult and children small groups and plans to add more. If Dean Hess had not defined Zion's history, he would have made far more mistakes.

Most churches are focused on events, staff, and mature leaders. This must change as you become a group-based church. If you continue to define success by attendance and "sizzle" at large events—Sunday school, women's fellowship, youth group—the church calendar will have little room for small groups. If laypeople still see themselves as objects of ministry, not ministers, and if they believe only the touch of paid staff counts, then small group shepherding will disappoint them. A church that entrusts a few jobs to the laity—ushering, greeting, teaching children—but reserves most leadership spots for a few good men (literally, in most places) will miss the chance for fundamental change.

## Where Are We Today?

Map your existing patterns of church life. You will cause less trauma wherever you can align current patterns to future design. Jim Dethmer, Willow's first small groups point leader, often said, "Groups are just a way to formalize what people are doing anyway."

University Baptist Church in Coral Gables, Florida, understands the importance of beginning where you are. When Mark Lesher began as pastor of adult life development, the church had a weekly attendance of almost 2,000, with 550 to 600 adults in traditional Sunday school classes.

"We weren't content that Sunday school was effecting discipleship. We realized that as our church was growing larger, it had to grow smaller," Lesher says. While moving toward Adult Bible Fellowship (ABF) small groups, he faced resistance in the seventy-five-year-old church. "What's going to happen to my Sunday school?" "Why are you throwing away our history?"

"People effectively labored for years in Sunday school. As we transition, we remind them of the continuity between the old model and ABF: our church is biblical, relational, family-oriented," Lesher says. In the ABF system, each room has a coach and five groups. A master teacher leads the first part of class, then small groups discuss the lesson. As the church ran out of meeting space, Lesher also introduced home groups.

University Baptist now has 500 adults in Sunday school, half in ABF small groups. Another 250 adults are in home groups, which means about two-thirds of adults are in groups. The children's ministry is also moving into small groups.

Lesher advises churches to ask for help, to pray, and to be patient. "We've had help from Pantego Bible Church, from Willow Creek, and from Spanish River. We were amazed how willing people were to help. They saw things we couldn't see. And don't underestimate the power of prayer. Our own spiritual formation as leaders makes the difference."

University Baptist did not change quickly and, in fact, is still in transition. "Raising the value on close relationships scares people. Many times I've thought this will never work. But God keeps saying, 'Your obedience is what matters. Keep going.' We can't settle for pseudo-transformation. We want groups where people feel cherished, where they step into the biblical story and discover it as their own. We want groups that share life together and live life in the name of Jesus," Lesher says.

Lesher has wisely taken what was already happening at University Baptist to bring a more holistic church approach to small groups. As we have seen at Willow and elsewhere, though, sometimes asking where you are now will lead you to stop doing certain things. You will notice that some activities at the whole-church or subministry levels actually block small group growth.

## What Are Our Core Values?

Before group life can become a church norm, your congregation needs six values. If it lacks any of the following core values, you will have trouble diffusing a pervasive small group model:

- *Building relationships.* How much do parishioners naturally care for each other?
- *Loving lost people.* Are people inclined toward outsiders?
- *Truth-telling.* Does your congregation acknowledge and deal with conflict?
- *Mutual ministry.* What is the current lay ministry quotient?
- *Accountability.* Is there enough vulnerability and submission to grow?
- *Commitment.* Do people own the church's mission and act like it?

## Who Influences Decisions in Our Church?

Whether you can become a group-based church depends on the senior pastor and on how change happens in your congregation. *You will not build a church of small groups unless the senior pastor endorses and fully lives out the vision.* Key church leaders can make a tremendous difference in carrying out a new strategy. But it is the senior pastor who carries the power of the pulpit, provides cues to the congregation on what matters most, models the preferred life of the church, and calls people to get involved. If you are a senior pastor reading this, then remember: you influence decisions more than you know.

You can learn a lot by studying how key leaders influence change.[1] Although described with variable terminology, students of change process concur on the critical role of the "early adopter" or "pioneer" group in any setting. Those who change first disproportionately influence those who follow. If the formal and informal influencers in your congregation become small group pioneers, you will find success sooner. The same group's resistance may stymie the decision to build a church of small groups.

### How Will We Craft and Articulate a Vision to Our Key Leadership?

Here are two reality checks on whether you are ready to move toward small groups. First, thoroughly describe your small group design in writing. Second, field questions from key church leaders.

Putting your proposal on paper is possible if you have designed a long-range plan, determined how to deploy many new leaders, and defined your core values. As Vineyard founder John Wimber once said, "Thoughts disentangle themselves as they flow through the tip of a pen." Asking for feedback further refines your thinking. If you keep a posture of open discussion while moving in concentric circles through varied leadership groups, you'll receive increased wisdom. Every time a key leader points out a flaw, you have a chance to avoid a costly consequence.

Seeking input from varied audiences will build ownership as well. You will discover natural resistance points. By moving stakeholders through awareness, familiarity, anticipation, and ownership, you will learn what the change process will take for the whole congregation. This is one time the process will be better than the outcome.

### What Are Potential Resources and Barriers?

Assess whether you have enough leaders and potential leaders, finances, training, equipment, staff, consultants, forums for conversation, and facilities. Willow Creek and other churches have found how important it is especially to face financial implications. Funding an extensive small group ministry costs more when you start, but costs drop as the infrastructure matures. At first, you will need paid staff to help identify, recruit, train, develop, and support small group leaders and coaches. Think of the significant initial cost as priming the pump for long-term ministry.

Now that Willow has developed and commissioned a sizeable volunteer army, we find that laypeople want to do more and are uniquely gifted and ready for distinctive ministry involvement. Some coaches have been leading leaders for a decade. As they reach professional and economic stability and no longer need to earn as much, some become bivocational, splitting time between paid work and ministry. As we give away more ministries to them, they respond in remarkable ways. Unpaid staff fill roles previously held by paid staff or new ones for which we would have needed to hire someone. The trend line continues to improve as we project forward, so we will have relatively reduced cost to sustain the infrastructure.

Ironically, one of the greatest barriers you have today may become the best resource for tomorrow. When you face financial hurdles, take the long-term investment view.

## How Should We Repurpose Existing Meetings to Include Group Life?

Whenever we discuss building a church of small groups, people ask, "How do you deal with leaders' schedules?" Parents enroll their kids in and taxi them to too many activities. Adults respond to work pressures by seeking expensive leisure. The time it takes to eat out, fill up, call in, check out, make up, and tune in eclipses the church's call for minimal discipleship. As former Harvard business school professor Len Schlessinger observed at the 1998 Willow Creek Leadership Summit, "Who is the church's competitor? Every alternative use of time." That is stiff competition.

Churches that reckon with the current reality of people's lives and modify the church calendar accordingly will prevail. You must find ways to serve leaders and members and empathize with their calendars. Once you are serving people in their current situation, you will have built the trust to confront poor time investment patterns. Eventually, you can mentor someone into better life choices, but you must meet them on their terms first.

Church staff members tend to be overscheduled, preoccupied with activities many laypeople consider marginal. Be considerate of their needs; don't call a meeting unless you have a clear purpose and worthwhile content. Leverage current attendance patterns by shifting what you do when people come to the church. Here are ways we have tried to take our message to the lay leaders:

- *Use our mid-week New Community services* to address and honor leaders.
- *Send quarterly cassette tapes* that commuters can play in cars; we may start sending CDs, too.
- *Explore technology-based training* for leaders to use when they have time.

- *Schedule meetings at times when people are already on campus,* even if we have to sacrifice the amount of content or spread communication over several meetings.
- *Rely on ministry areas* to communicate a centralized, coordinated message when their participants are already present.

Unless we who are paid to serve the congregation connect our world to theirs, we will fail to see where current reality needs change. Let's stop bemoaning the competition and make authentic efforts toward fresh process and substance.

## What Are the Implications for Our Staff?

"We are going to have to turn over one-third of our staff to achieve the goal of becoming a church of small groups," I (Russ) prophesied to Bill Hybels in 1995. In evaluating our transition strategy, I had discovered that 40 percent of the congregation was in a small group. One barrier to progress seemed to be that most of our staff had been hired to do a job other than small groups. Before 1992, we employed people to deliver the goods to others, not through others. Since then we had worked around staff members who didn't have the gifts or passion to make community part of their personal ministry. I thought we had too many old dogs to teach new tricks.

By 2000, we had 90 percent of our church in groups, and almost every staff member was leading some aspect of community life. I'm happy to say I was wrong. We didn't have to fire one-third of our staff and replace them with the right people. Some staff members discovered a knack for small group duties, which, in retrospect, makes sense. All of them had been hired because they had a heart to serve. Many had leadership or shepherding gifts, ones that required simple redirection. Once they got past ordinary resistance to change, most actually liked their increased impact on people. Some staff feared their modified job descriptions, but they did well once we delivered training and support.

As the small group movement spread, it became more normal for everyone, staff and volunteers alike, to do groups. A handful of staff members chose to leave because they enjoyed delivering ministry more than equipping others for it. We allowed the processing to take adequate time, but also did not shy away from making the hard call to let them go. Whether you redirect a mature church or begin a church with a small groups foundation, every staff member must lead the way.

At New Community Church in Wexford, Pennsylvania, small groups have been a core value since it began two years ago. "The key value we've hammered from the beginning is transformation," says Reichart, Small Groups Pastor. "That top value is supported by two foundational values: small communities and biblical truth."

The start-up church has small groups and serving groups; its seven coaches are also board members. "We have tried to make our coaches our best leaders," Reichart says. The senior pastor, Hollis Haff, another teaching pastor, Mark Bolton, and Reichart are all heavily involved in shepherding small group leaders. "It's an important value, so we wanted to have the senior leadership involved," Reichart says. "That's where our heart is."

■

It's worth the investment to navigate all five forks on the path to becoming a church of small groups. You will face hard decisions about whether your church will become a church of small groups, who will lead, how it will look, what leaders will be needed, and where you are. But you will see the fruit of wise decisions over time. Ask for help from churches already on this path. Their experiences will help you choose a strategy for basing your church on well-planned community.

# Choose a Strategy

*Here is where we must begin just like Jesus. It will be slow, tedious, painful, and probably unnoticed by people at first, but the end result will be glorious, even if we don't live to see it. Seen this way, though, it becomes a big decision in the ministry.*
ROBERT COLEMAN, *MASTER PLAN OF EVANGELISM*

I (Russ) am an incurable baseball-aholic. I got hooked as a young boy, the first time I watched Harmon Killebrew and the Minnesota Twins. The Twins almost won the World Series in 1965, and they were *my* team—until I moved to North Dakota, where I became an Atlanta Braves fan. The Braves were our hometown team, because theirs were the only games on "The Superstation WTBS" cable broadcasts. I'm still a Braves addict, despite living in Chicago. Here, faced with a choice between the White Sox or the Cubs—a rivalry that pits otherwise friendly people in community-busting conflict—I keep my local loyalties to myself.

Watching three teams for years, I've seen how they tailor their unique approach to the game. Some teams rely on great pitching to win; others are built for speed. Power hitters dominate some line-ups, while some teams focus on defense and execution to win. The approach will be based on team history, stadium location and type, managerial preference, and the players' natures and abilities.

Just as a baseball team must choose a strategy for good team play, so must a church. To extend the metaphor, once you decide to become a group-based church, you are ready to play the game. You own a team, have picked the manager, know what you want it to look like in the long run, have a plan to develop players, and see where your team is today.

But for long-term success, you still have to choose a core strategy for growing groups—for team play.

We won't pull punches with you. Your strategy will require common language that may feel uncomfortably corporate, since vision and church organizing meet here in redemptive mission. But behind the strategies and structures are the transformed lives of women, men, children, and families. As Bill Hybels often tells our team, "Listen, if my lost friend has just found Christ and needs to be shepherded in a small group, I *want* this thing to be organized to the zenith of its potential!" When lives and eternities are at stake, strategy matters.

Though Willow Creek grows groups using Carl George's metachurch model, other churches base their small group infrastructure on the cell church model, defined in part by Ralph Neighbor, or on newer models, such as G-12 or free-market cells. The method you select will depend on your setting, leadership, people, history, and other church issues.

No matter which model you choose, you will be most successful if your strategy includes these six core principles: organize around span of care, advocate open groups, vary and align ministry, create a leadership culture, cultivate intentionality, and contextualize your approach.

## Organize around Span of Care

Nobody—even a leader as gifted as Moses—can violate the span of care principle for long without burning out. Any church that violates span of care becomes unable to retain and care for people. Your growth model must make sure everyone is cared for, but nobody cares for too many. Span of care includes choosing a healthy group size, being willing to birth new groups, choosing new coaches, and finding ways to support coaches.

How many is too many in a small group? As metachurch disciples, we have used the 1:10 ratio from Exodus 18, though we have made exceptions. A leader with near-Messiah ability may be able to care for twelve people, as Christ did, but people have trouble feeling known and celebrated in larger groups. Our current experience suggests that a 1:8 ratio may be healthier. When groups grow beyond eight members, individuals don't get enough time to share. They become less inclined to vulnerability, less effective in meeting other members' needs. Leaders choose between burnout or self-preservation as they try to care for each member. We are noticing that as societal dysfunction increases, care gets more challenging. Smaller groups may be better.

Birthing is the natural process of healthy small groups. Over time, groups attract new members. It's not uncommon for a group to swell to fifteen or twenty members, simply because God is at work through a leader or in a little community. But unless leaders and members expect their group to birth another, Jethro's words to Moses will forever haunt them: "You and these people who come to you will only wear yourselves out" (Exodus 18:18).

In churches just beginning to grow groups, the point leader often provides care for small group leaders. As their numbers soar, the point leader soon needs to recruit coaches, those who care for small group leaders. "One of our biggest mistakes was not putting enough emphasis on coaching," says Gary Foran of Kensington Community Church. "We tried to get people to do 'a little bit of coaching,' but nobody was interested. They saw it as just checking up on other group leaders and having to give up leading groups. We needed to cast a bigger vision so coaches would see developing other leaders as their ministry."

Like Gary Foran, we at Willow Creek learned that good leaders don't necessarily make good coaches. The jobs require different skills. A small group leader may be remarkably gifted in shepherding, but without a proven leadership gift, that same person won't be as effective at coaching.

Mike Skor also understands the coaching challenge. Before recently joining the River Church in Sacramento, California, as the small groups point leader, Mike was director of small groups at Daybreak Community Church in Hudsonville, Michigan. When Skor came to Daybreak five years ago, it was a seeker-oriented, culturally relevant church—with a few adult small groups. He now has four coaches and thirty groups in a church with weekend attendance of about 600 adults and 250 children. There are fifty more groups within the student and children's ministries. He meets monthly with his four coaches and says, "The biggest win for us has been realizing how important coaches are. I need four more coaches right now, but they're hard to find. Still, I think setting the bar high for the coaching position is the best move we've made."

As your church develops more small group leaders and coaches, the point leader will need help caring for coaches. You can either hire a new staff person or develop lay senior coaches. At Willow Creek, we've hired new staff (called division leaders) to oversee every ten coaches. We made this substantial staff investment so we could catalyze our small group infrastructure without violating span of care.

In the future, we will probably choose instead to deploy lay senior coaches. Just as a coach leads small group leaders, a senior coach leads three to five lay coaches, thus extending the ultimate span of care for the point leader or other staff. Since these laypeople carry significant congregational leadership responsibility—shepherding 150 to 250 people—they truly become bivocational. Our early experiments are yielding favorable results.

Be sure to make span of care part of your strategy. Otherwise your church will suffer leader burnout, subgroup cliques, increased group conflict, and group dissension caused by unmet needs.

## Advocate Open Groups

There are two laws of spiritual entropy. The first law, as Willow Creek's Mark Mittelberg explains, is loss of evangelistic relationships, the statistically proven trend for new believers to shed unchurched friends within twelve months. The second law is to hoard community. A Christian who has found a fulfilling small group instinctively wants to protect that rare prize. Building a church of small groups collides with both laws.

Though starting new groups is the main way churches become group based, most growth models also include a mechanism for adding people to existing groups. However, we have learned that open groups must be a foundational, not an optional, principle in any strategy for becoming a church of small groups. *If you want to make group life normal for every person in your church, then the unconnected person must be free to choose from both new and open groups.* You'll achieve maximum connectivity through a whole-congregation posture of outstretched arms. This requires a catalytic mechanism that follows normal relational rhythms. Open-group advocacy assumes realistic expectations about group life spans and natural life cycles.

A catalytic mechanism is an action, not a value. Jim Collins, who with Jerry Porras wrote the best-seller *Built to Last*, explains that while wholesale strategy change sometimes yields a desired outcome, often a smaller, incremental, but catalytic action does the job better. For example, a company may value customer service above all else, but its unconditional refund for customer dissatisfaction is the catalytic mechanism for actually serving customers. It is the action, not the value, that produces the desired outcome.

At Willow Creek, our catalytic mechanism for connecting people into groups has been the "open chair," our adaptation of the metachurch "empty chair" principle. We've based retreats on the open chair concept. We've built the phrase into our small group leaders orientation, group covenants, and storytelling. Everyone understands that a group is not a group unless it has an open chair. Even when a little community goes for a long time without adding a new member, everyone knows it may happen soon.

When I (Russ) teach our church's membership class about small groups, I discuss the value of group life here, including how living out the "Group G value" means resisting the urge to hoard community. I have found that not everyone understands how the open chair works. Some group members worry the church will enforce the open chair by sending unconnected people—probably bizarre talk show alumni or axe murderers—to disrupt their blissful community.

I explain how the open chair follows normal relational rhythms. In a group I led, one member began introducing an unconnected friend to other group members. Over time, we socialized and were together at church services and events, so the whole group began to befriend this person. The new friend eventually visited the small group meeting. We realized his presence had become such a routine part of our relational network that it was time to fill our group's open chair.

Many Willow Creek leaders and groups rebelled against the open group principles until we helped them set realistic expectations for group life span. Most group models assume too short a life span. At first, optimal metachurch theory led us to teach that groups should fill the open chair and birth new groups every eighteen to twenty-four months. In some cell models, groups birth after six to nine months. We learned, however, that in our setting, most nontask-based groups (meeting approximately every other week) birth in thirty to thirty-six months. Even then, variations outnumber that rule of thumb.

Contrary to group models, many laypeople assume a good group will last into heaven. This false assumption prompts them to protect their permanent community by closing the group to new members. When groups recognize their probable life span, they will more likely remain open. Though some groups are lifelong, societal mobility limits most groups' duration. Fifteen years ago Lynn and I led a young couples group in which all of us grew, stretched, prayed, communicated, and loved as we never had before. We would have happily grown old and gray together. But three years after the group started, three of the five couples (including us) moved away.

Most groups follow a predictable lifecycle. They grow. They die. With growth come growing pains. With death comes grief. Over a period of fifty or so meetings, a group will be like a plant that cycles through growth spurts and stagnation. Ten years of living in North Dakota farm country taught me that the open chair is to groups what fertilizer is to crops. A group grows when a leader tends it and people give each other care. But, just as the right fertilizer, properly applied, stimulates crop growth, so a new person or couple fertilizes a group with new friendships, resources, and connections to a wider community. As in farming, the wrong additive can harm or destroy, but the risk is usually worth it for groups that trust God to work through their outstretched arms.

If you include open groups in your strategy, groups will be amazed at what God does through them. Open groups offer ever-expanding opportunities for people to connect with your church and for your groups and leaders to become even more fruitful.

## Vary and Align Ministry

How do you provide enough entry points for people while keeping everybody moving in the right direction? You vary group types to meet many needs, and you persuade staff and key leaders to align every ministry under a small groups infrastructure. This two-pronged principle is perhaps the toughest challenge in developing a church *of* groups strategy.

Willow Creek once had excellent but one-dimensional discipleship groups. These discipleship groups met our church's need to mature the faith of new Christians and move them into volunteerism and church leadership. In this "one size fits all" approach, a couple had to be married, make a two-year commitment to a group, attend three meetings a month, and seriously seek growth. Our discipleship program wasn't bad; it was simply too narrow to meet other needs.

Since we decided to become a church of small groups, I (Bill) have seen the benefit of focusing on people's needs and maturity levels. In the first years, we offered five kinds of groups (see chart).

## Five Major Types of Groups

|  | Disciple-Making Groups | Community Groups | Service Groups | Seeker Groups | Support Groups |
|---|---|---|---|---|---|
| **Members** | Believers seeking a structured discipleship process | Believers and nonbelievers | Believers and nonbelievers | Predominantly nonbelievers | Believers and nonbelievers |
| **Curriculum** | A set curriculum such as the *Walking with God* series by Zondervan | Leaders work with Coaches to choose curriculum | Leaders work with Coaches to choose curriculum | Determined by questions of members | Determined by ministry leaders |
| **Open Chair** | Used at breaks in curriculum | Used regularly to add members | Used regularly to add members | Always has an open chair | Used primarily to form new groups |
| **Emphasis** | Develop spiritual disciplines, memorize Scripture, disciple others | Build community, invite new members | Complete the task, invite new members | Lead people to Christ, disciple new converts | To support members as they work through personal difficulties |
| **Multiplication** | Apprentice leads new disciple-making group | Groups grow and birth after 24 to 36 months | Groups grow and birth at variable rates depending on the task | Apprentice leads new seeker group or new believers group | Apprentices are trained to form new groups |
| **Duration** | 18 to 24 months | Continue to grow and birth | Continue to grow and birth | Average length is about one year | Varies depending on personal needs and purpose of group |

Then we moved from five to infinity. Now that we offer any kind of group, according to need, we are much better at meeting people on their level of community readiness. We use people's longing for affinity—with others of like need, interest, or life stage—as an excuse to connect them. We also have groups for people who would rather experience a cross-section, meeting with, perhaps, a couple with children, a single mom, a college student, and empty nesters. We define a group as such when it has a qualified leader, one who assures people are connected to that leader and each other and who monitors the care and growth of the little community they represent.

Willow Creek's women's ministry has at least quintupled in size by varying its groups according to need. Diane Nobles, one of our elders, has experienced this increasing specialization. She's been in groups targeted to women, to women who are moms, to moms of tots, and to women who, like her, are working moms of tots. The niche focus helps us build a church of small groups that meets people where they are on their community readiness journey. A need provides us an excuse to get people together. Along the way, it becomes normal to be in a group.

Your church will have a similar opportunity as you choose a strategy. Some small group systems are more one-dimensional, offering higher control over group life, curriculum, activity, and outcome. Strategies allowing for varied affinities and cross-sectional connection are typically low-control structures; these require more monitoring, leader training, coaching, and leadership oversight. The more you vary your groups, the more people you will connect through felt needs for growth and community.

## From Splintered to Aligned

Our congregation is now cooperating in becoming a church of small groups since our members won in the process. But many of our staff and key leaders resisted the call to align their ministries under a small groups infrastructure. At Willow Creek, we have never started a ministry unless we had a called, anointed leader in place, whether paid or unpaid. We have rarely had to abandon efforts because of lack of leadership, nor find new people for vacant leadership slots. This "called and anointed" policy gave us loyal leaders with a high sense of ministry ownership. While we were a church *with* groups, these leaders could chart their own organizational courses.

But some strong leaders with deep passions and expertise began viewing their ministry as an end in itself rather than an organic part of a biblical body. We have a term for this dynamic of unhealthy independence—"splintering." In some sense, we became an association of parachurch ministries housed at one location. Moving those splintered ministries and their leaders toward group-based ministry took our leadership's best diplomacy.

Aligning every ministry under a common small groups infrastructure is the rubber-meets-the-road test of your church's resolve to become a church of small groups. No matter how well you execute the change, some people will label it a "top-down" imposition. When you choose a strategy, you will be choosing a strategy for each of your church's ministries as well. You must choose what will work well in a fully aligned enterprise.

Mary and Paul Schaller, coministers of small groups at Menlo Park Presbyterian Church in densely populated northern California, learned to meet the alignment challenge head-on. When they were hired, the church had many (no one knew how many) groups, but none were connected to the church or each other. Similarly, the church departments "were like silos: self-contained, self-sufficient, but not connected," Mary Schaller said.

The Schallers were hired to connect every ministry through a small group strategy and structure that would care for and develop leaders. Mary Schaller spent the first year tracking down the church's four hundred groups and building a database of groups and contact people.

She found a hundred groups for children and thirty-five for singles. Each of those ministries had, independent of the church or each other, set up a metamodel for their small groups, with leaders, apprentices, coaches, and training. There were program-related groups, such as Mothers Together, which met at church for large-group teaching, then broke into smaller groups. Menlo Park had scores of groups for men, women, and couples, many led by leaders with no support or connection to the church.

The Schallers invited leaders to join official "growth groups," so they could get help finding new members and coaches. Next they invited some of the strongest leaders to attend a nine-week "coaches circle," where they studied the Willow Creek Coaches Handbook. "The Spirit is moving here, because people are willing to do things that seem counter-intuitive but really do work," Mary said. Coaches-circle graduates have been assigned groups. New leaders circles train small group leaders.

Menlo Park Presbyterian serves a wide geographic area. "Years ago, the area was divided into fifty-six parishes, each assigned to two deacons, usually a married couple. But the church never put resources into caring for those 120 deacons, so they weren't very effective," Mary said. Now the church is hiring eleven regional associates, who will act as regional pastor for five or six parishes and provide support for deacons. Within regions, deacons will be freed to serve according to their spiritual gifts rather than geography; at least one deacon in each region will be a small group liaison.

"This process would have been easier if our church had no small groups and we could start from scratch. Some of our groups are doing great. Others are 'news, sports, and weather.' They're not growing in their faith, but we're working on it," Mary said.

## Four Lessons for Ministry Alignment

As Menlo Park Presbyterian and Willow Creek have experienced, leaders sometimes resist the move toward a group-based church. We learned four lessons about moving from resistance to advocacy.

First, *communication is critical*. We failed to communicate adequately with leaders of the "church with" version of small groups. We didn't explain often enough or deeply enough about how they would fit within the new infrastructure. Instead of building on our strong foundation, we alienated a key audience—then had to win them back.

Second, *stay flexible*. Whatever strategy you choose needs a "loose-tight balance." You need a uniform set of standards and definitive understanding of what constitutes group life and what does not. Yet, the ministry-by-ministry expression of groups must permit increased variety in meeting every person's need and readiness for community.

Third, *balance patience with relentlessness*. It took us seven years to organize every part of the church on a full small groups foundation. Sometimes we made partial gains, backed off until change was accepted, then returned to chip away again. As a Zion Lutheran leader observed, "We are in year twelve of a twenty-year vision, and we are going to have to extend it beyond that." Alignment takes time.

Finally, *confrontation is essential*. We have been a truth-telling community, one that does not shy away from discussing change. We directly engaged with ministry leaders as we worked through the chaos of aligning their strategy to be group based. When resistance set in, we named it and then lovingly went after it.

We freely admit that varying group types to meet many needs takes work. It's even harder to persuade staff and key leaders to align every ministry under a small groups infrastructure. Working both elements into your strategy will be a good news/bad news story; however, persistence will pay off in a happy ending.

## Create a Leadership Culture

Every small group ministry model depends on leaders. Yet most churches are not leader-oriented. They see humility and invisibility as more God-pleasing than high-impact leaders who take the platform of influence. In our experience, your chosen strategy will be more effective if you intensify your focus on leadership. You can create a leadership culture by defining servant leadership, teaching the priesthood of believers, and expecting leaders to be effective.

### Spiritual Leadership

In the church, people are permitted only one approach to leadership—servanthood. Leadership is a function of needs and gifts, not hierarchy and importance. Need is the primary driver of servanthood, even when no leader is particularly gifted. In the Bible, people were asked to lead in response to community need. We see this in Jethro's suggestion to Moses and in the early church's response to neglected widows.

If your potential leadership pool is larger than you need, then you can screen for spiritual gifts, calling, capability, and readiness. Those with leadership gifts will lead best in the biblical paradigm. These leaders deserve credit only for being faithful to God by using their gifts to benefit his body. Any leader who loses heart because he or she isn't getting enough recognition or affirmation is wrestling with character issues or missing what the Bible says about stewardship of gifts.

### The Priesthood of Believers

Creating a leadership culture hinges, in part, on seeing everyone in your congregation as a potential leader. Talk about and to these leaders by practically embedding the doctrine of the priesthood of all believers. In *The New Reformation*, Greg Ogden explains:

We are all priests in that we minister directly before God. The one high priest Jesus Christ has opened the way to God by presenting himself as the sacrifice for our sin, and he sits at God's right hand to make intercession for us continually. A special class of priests representing us to God and God to us is no longer needed. We are all drawn into the priesthood in that we represent ourselves before God through the covering of the mediator, Jesus Christ.

The unfinished business and the unkept promise that has the power to unleash a grass-roots revolution is the logical corollary to the priesthood of all believers. For not only are all believers priests before God, we also are all priests to each other and in the world.[1]

Every person is a priest, given a ministry in the church; yet, qualifications do matter. One of the oxymoronic phrases in small group ministry is "leaderless groups." A leaderless group is either in denial, because someone is the de facto leader, or will be dysfunctional for the little time it lasts. A group's quality depends most of all on its leader. Becoming a group-based church is directly correlated to the strength of its leadership.

## Expectations for Effective Leaders

As you build a leadership culture, clearly state your expectations for effective leaders. Define their gifts, competencies, role requirements, spiritual qualifications, and character traits. Build a church-wide expectation that being in leadership means regularly assessing current effectiveness to define the next growth steps. Reward excellence with affirmation, then increased ministry influence and opportunity. Confront leadership failures or deficiencies with grace and a spirit of learning. Help people see church leadership as an esteemed lifestyle choice or, as one of our leaders puts it, "not for a year but a career."

People will respond to such a high calling. Rather than shrink back because the cost is too high, the best leaders will lean into the opportunities you offer. They will thrive as long as they are growing and you are investing in them.

## Cultivate Intentionality

While becoming a church of small groups, Willow Creek was obsessed with connecting every person into a caring community. We leveraged aggressive leadership placement, group variety, open chairs, and span of care to retrofit groups into a multifaceted church. It worked, but it cost us. Group quality sometimes suffered. Some leaders were ill-prepared. Some teams focused so much on ministry tasks, such as ushering or childcare, that their jobs defeated community.

Guaranteeing everyone is connected and cared for is hard enough. Harder still is growing groups that intentionally disciple and develop people. Intentionality means that leaders help build a church of small groups by being systematically devoted to moving people to spiritual maturity. Small groups provide the greenhouse for methodically tending life-changing fruit. Leaders intentionally form authentic relationships so they can help people assess whether God's Word is transforming them. Leaders help group members resolve conflicts and balance discipling and caring. You can cultivate intentionality by creating a common language, integrating systems, and providing tools for leaders.

## Creating Common Language

It's essential to create a common language that will unite people from varied church backgrounds. I (Russ) learned this the hard way when I was asked to oversee directly five of our church's ministries. I pulled the ministry point leaders together and asked what seemed to me a simple question: "How would a person behave if they were living out Willow Creek's ideal of being a fully devoted follower of Christ?" Seven meetings later, we were still talking. Each leader had his or her own language—the Campus Crusade view, Navigators lingo, Skyline/John Maxwell ideas—to describe spiritual growth.

Leaders remained polite, but each saw his or her own approach as right and the others as deficient. Most churches experience this disharmony of terms. Christendom has created terrific discipleship systems, but these separate successes make it harder to agree on a common language and approach. Through hard work, the point leaders and I gradually let go of old language and agreed on uniform terms to incorporate churchwide. Being intentional about language has enhanced communication, reduced confusion, and unified leadership.

The terms we now use to help people describe their spiritual progress are grace, growth, groups, gifts, and good stewardship—"the 5 Gs" described in chapter 7. No language adequately expresses discipleship, and these terms may not work in your setting. But unless you choose uniform language, your church will have less chance to intentionally help people grow through small groups.

## Integrating Systems

Even after choosing a group-based strategy, most churches will continue to have other ministries or systems. For example, at Willow Creek we integrated our membership strategy with the 5 Gs, so membership materials could drive spiritual change. We see membership as a core spiritual development process; people study a curriculum, self-assess, address growth needs, promise commitment, and renew their membership every three years.

Because a person's leader best knows his or her true spiritual condition, we put our small group leadership in charge of membership. When initially affirmed as a member, a person is interviewed by her small group leader and that leader's coach. When she renews her membership, her small group leader affirms her continued 5 Gs progress. If the leader isn't sure, the coach gets involved. Integrating membership with small group strategy gives leaders the chance to be more intentional in helping people become devoted to Christ.

## Providing Tools for Leaders

We provide leaders with tools for intentional growth, such as the *Pursuing Spiritual Transformation* small group curriculum. This entry-level study set helps leaders orient a group to the underlying biblical principles for the 5Gs. Another tool is the "Shepherding Plan" mentioned in chapter 7. We have created several variations on this tool so leaders can purposefully plan the next month's group and individual advancement. Again, there is nothing magic in the particular language, systems, or tools, *but rather that you cultivate intentionality in your chosen strategy.*

# Contextualize Your Approach

The term "contextualization" makes people think of Hudson Taylor's adopting Chinese dress, customs, and language so he could proclaim the gospel in a new culture. It's time to think of community-building in the same way. Little communities—small groups—are the means of creating transforming, authentic relationships. But how we make such groups available to our people and integrate them into the larger framework of church life requires church leaders to consider their unique setting and culture. Spanish River Presbyterian in Boca Raton, Florida, and Pantego Bible Church in Arlington, Texas, know how to contextualize.

Spanish River learned that if the shoe doesn't fit, don't wear it. "You have to contextualize what you've got," explains Gary Treichler, executive pastor and previous associate of Lyman Coleman at Serendipity Ministries. Treichler learned Carl George's metachurch strategy as a Small Groups Pastor at Grace Fellowship in Baltimore, Maryland, where Jim Dethmer (who in 1991 cast Willow Creek's church *of* groups vision) was senior pastor. Groups were "a way of life" at Grace.

"This is the most different place I've ever done ministry," Treichler says of southern Florida. "Things were just not working as they did in Baltimore. So many people read *Prepare Your Church for the Future* and think, 'This is exactly how we have to do it.' But simply copying a model is ill-fated."

Spanish River Church (SRC) decentralized the vision-casting element. It hired only people with a passion for small groups, such as Suzanne Jeansonne, who began as the senior pastor's administrative assistant. Three years ago, Treichler realized Jeansonne had the gifts of administration and visionary leadership as well as a passion for connecting SRC's 1,500 attendees into small groups. She had been working behind the scenes in women's ministries and readily accepted when Treichler asked her to reorganize the ministry into small groups, which now number about 250.

Her ministry now connects over 350 women through thirty-five Tuesday morning and twelve Wednesday evening groups. Six teachers take turns leading large-group times, then women break into small groups to discuss a curriculum written by Jeansonne and her team. Her leader-training sessions incorporate teaching, drama, and vision casting. Her solid structure includes an apprentice leader for every group, group leaders, and coaches. "I love it," says Jeansonne. "It took a long time to get it working the way it should, but it's worth it."

What works for women hasn't worked for men, Treichler admits. "It's harder to do the training. We're starting to put more emphasis on fishing ponds (assimilation events), and we form many small groups out of such gatherings."

SRC's youth ministry is cell-based. The church also has a support group ministry; with permission its point leader tweaked a small group model and trained his own people. Spanish River is becoming a church of small groups because Treichler believes in letting each staff member adapt and contextualize the small groups vision.

In *The Connecting Church*, Randy Frazee, pastor of Pantego Bible Church, explains how his church repositioned itself to build true community. Though the church had made groups a top value and people readily joined affinity groups (men, women, life stages, etc.), they weren't being transformed. Its nineteen Sunday school classes met regularly but experienced little lasting spiritual growth.

Pantego Bible Church is in Arlington, Texas, a city of 350,000 people in metro Dallas-Fort Worth. Weekend attendance (about 2,500 adults and 1,000 children) draws from a large area. Thus, unless they happen to live in the same neighborhood, members don't often see each other outside church. Pantego realized that reorganizing groups by neighborhood would make it easier for group members to really "do life together." They now have about a thousand people in eighty-three groups.

The church replaced Sunday school with twenty-seven medium-sized community groups made up of people in the same public high school district. Each community group includes three to five "home groups." Home groups meet in homes during the week and are made up of seven to seventeen people in the same junior high or elementary school district.

"We chose geography because we want more touches per week," says Bill Barnett, director of small groups. He notes that if groups only meet twice a month and people don't live near each other, building intimacy takes longer. Because many home group members live on the same street or in the same apartment complex, they "come close" to the Acts 2:42 reality of daily fellowship. According to Barnett, "The normal time to get to intimacy in a group is about nine months. With these groups, it happens in about four months. By intimacy, I mean a willingness to discuss what's really going on."

Pantego's staff has four geographic zone pastors, each in charge of five to ten community groups. The church uses interns from nearby Dallas Seminary or Southwestern Baptist Theological Seminary as apprentice zone pastors. One pastor oversees the singles ministry, which transcends geography. The singles are evenly split between regular home groups and singles groups. Pantego also sponsors about thirty foreign missionaries, with two or three groups assigned to pray for and send letters, e-mail, and care packages to missionaries.

It would be easier if one model worked well for every church, but you know it doesn't. Consciously choose to contextualize your approach, whether you have to organize groups around geography or affinity or adapt them to unique cultural traits. As many churches have discovered, it's challenging—but entirely possible—to move members into authentic community while remaining laser focused on the mission.

## Championships Depend on a Choice

There are no shortcuts to becoming a church of small groups, just as there is no easy way to build a World Series team. It requires a decision to make it happen, then a strategy to make it real. You will not happen to become a church of small groups more than any team happens to win.

Strategy does matter. You have to know what you are trying to achieve and how you will make it happen so you can communicate compellingly. People will respond in proportion to the conviction with which they are invited. Progress can only be measured against a known set of parameters. You can shift methodology along the way as you learn, but there must be a standard against which learning is measured. Once the strategy is working, you can celebrate its success with those who helped make it happen.

In small group ministry, your strategy must account for span of care. Open groups will aid your journey. Varied entry points will give everyone ways to connect in an aligned ministry. A self-perpetuating leadership corps will grow into shepherding the whole flock effectively, especially as you intentionally cultivate spiritual growth and contextualize your growth model.

# Phasing in the Small Group Ministry

*When we come home at the end of the day, it may not be just work we bring with us, but also our high-speed frustrations and electronic expectations. In short, we may come to expect the imperfect human beings in our lives to operate as efficiently as our equipment, quickly losing patience with those we might otherwise love because they do not answer as swiftly, or respond as rapidly, or obey as readily as the machines we know.*

STEPHEN BERTMAN, *HYPERCULTURE*

When you begin to build a church of small groups, incredible things will happen. Every single member of your church will catch and fully embrace a new vision for community. Every person with leadership potential will surrender gifts and abilities to the cause. Groups will pop up faster than you can count them. Elders, board members, long-time church attendees, and the choir leader will rise up and call you blessed. Sins will be renounced. Full-time employees will intentionally taper to part-time, so they can volunteer twenty or thirty hours a week to help build this ministry. Giving will increase 200 percent, and international ministry will quadruple. Lost people will come to faith in every small group that starts. Life will never be the same!

If you believe anything that we just said, it's time to say no to drugs. The only thing that is totally true in the last paragraph is that *life will never be the same*. We wish we could promise total success when you seek to become a church of small groups. Reality teaches us otherwise. We cannot tell you how fast this new vision will take root; we cannot predict that most people will embrace the change enthusiastically; we cannot promise that you will have more leaders than you ever imagined.

We can be sure, however, that your ministry will progress through phases as you seek to build a church of small groups. Though the length and intensity of each phase may vary, we are convinced that small group ministry progresses through fairly predictable stages. It's a lot like life. Most eighty-year-olds had a childhood and somewhat bumpy adolescence; then, during their twenties and thirties they learned what they did or didn't do well. They made mid-course corrections in their forties and fifties, had time to reflect and develop wisdom during their sixties and seventies, and know death will come. But predictability doesn't necessarily mean boring. Is your life boring? Ours aren't.

Small group ministry may have predictable phases, but we believe it's one of the greatest ministry adventures you'll ever experience. Your church will go through model/turbo, pilot, and start-up phases before you "go public" with small groups. Though the particulars of each phase will depend on your church context, you will find that certain general principles apply.

## The Model/Turbo Group Phase

The best way to embed community values into small group ministry is to model them yourself. If your church is just beginning small groups, start with a few model groups, led (ideally) by the senior pastor and/or other key church leaders. Choosing and living out important values gives you high control over the character and nature of the small groups you launch. In the modeling phase, you can experiment with your own growth in community and discover together how a small group really should function.

Turbo groups ratchet up the model group concept. Turbo groups are small groups filled with apprentice leaders. In other words, everyone in the group is expected to someday lead his or her own group. Thus, a turbo group functions as both a real small group and a training group.

As a church moves toward becoming a church of small groups, it often tries out several models for small group structure, such as the cell model, the meta model, or even the example of another church perceived as successful. But, as Shakespeare advised, "To thine own self be true." Each church needs to adapt models to its own context.

For example, in the 1970s, a forward-thinking pastor implemented small groups, coaches, and overseers at Christian Assembly (C.A.) in Los

Angeles, California. But by the early 1990s, attendance at worship was below two hundred and no groups remained. In recent years, the century-old church has tried several models. "They failed one after the other," admits Mark Guzman, Small Groups Pastor.

He and Pastor Mark Pickerel decided that they needed more information to make small groups work, so they attended Willow Creek's Church Leaders Conference in 1997. "We did the small group track," Guzman recalls. "We were overwhelmed. Weekend services now draw 2,500 people, and a thousand wanted to be in small groups. We didn't know how to do it. After Bill Donahue visited us to consult on small groups—we were even more overwhelmed!"

Deciding to retry the meta model, they developed a turbo group of ten couples with leadership potential, which met for seven months. After a summer break, Guzman identified another 150 leaders within the church. "We sent them a high-vision, high-challenge letter outlining our dream for small groups," he says. For ten weeks that fall, they provided dinner, childcare, and training to about ninety leaders on small group values, such as the open chair, apprentices, multiplying groups, and mission.

Though C.A. needed several attempts to design its ministry model, notice that it used turbo groups to form the small groups ministry foundation. The church began to experience success when it focused on coaching and leadership training. Unless you use the model/turbo phase to identify emerging coaches and think seriously about their roles, your church will be overwhelmed too.

The model/turbo phase emphasizes values, small group life, and initial training for your first group of leaders. These groups are ready to birth when leaders feel fully prepared to lead their own groups. Some leaders pair up to launch new groups. That's okay, but we'd rather that each turbo group member choose an apprentice from outside the group, then recruit members to their own new group.

The following guidelines will help your turbo groups succeed:

- *Turbo groups must build authentic community.* This is not simply a training group. These people must understand and practice community or they will never reproduce it in their own groups.
- *Turbo groups must experience all components of a regular group.* They need to practice the open chair, identify apprentice leaders, create places where truth meets life, build authentic relationships,

and appropriately handle conflict—so that the same things will take place in the next set of groups.

- *Turbo groups must seize teachable moments.* In these groups, leadership lessons are often caught, not taught. It is appropriate in the context of a turbo group to pause and say, "Let's talk about what just happened—and why—in the last ten minutes." Or, leaders might ask, "Why did I do this? What did you see me doing that was good or needs improving?"

- *Turbo groups take time.* Turbo groups probably need at least nine to twelve months to appropriately train new leaders. It can happen more quickly if the group meets weekly or if leaders have prior small group experience. However, brand new leaders may need as long as eighteen to twenty-four months of preparation.

## The Pilot Group Phase

After firmly establishing your core values and clarifying your small group development model, you are ready for the pilot group phase. This is a learning phase for a limited number of groups. New to the nature and meaning of small group community, many people will be wary of long-term commitments. During this phase, you start a limited number of small groups that last just nine to twelve months. The time limit is a safety net; it gives everyone a chance to pause, evaluate, and redesign.

Willow Creek first piloted small groups in our couples and singles ministries. This trial-and-error phase let us see how small groups worked in our local church context. You must do the same step. At this point, inviting everyone at church to join a small group could be disastrous. Most churches are not ready to connect the masses into groups. You need the pilot group phase to make sure leaders are well-trained and groups are working as hoped.

In churches that already have groups, piloting may mean a fresh start or second chance to make small groups work. For example, when Brenda Rizor accepted leadership of a small groups ministry at First Wesleyan in Battle Creek, Michigan, she says God kept reminding her, "You already have it."

Although the number of groups in the church has grown from forty to 164 during Rizor's two years on staff, she credits the foundation already in place. Senior Pastor Robert Nicholson has been a big part of

First Wesleyan's push to become a church of small groups. "He's behind small groups, and he's in a group himself," Rizor says. "He's been casting a vision for small groups for six years." The church has 1,500 adults and children attending three services.

Rizor built on the strengths of the original forty groups. First Wesleyan's several twelve-step recovery groups gave her a model for raising up new leaders. "Wednesday Night Live" was a thriving children's ministry based on small groups. When adults cited lack of childcare as a barrier to joining small groups, Rizor realized she could piggyback adult groups onto the successful children's ministries.

As a result, about 150 adults now meet in groups at church on Wednesday nights. While their kids enjoy drama, music, and small group time, the adults watch a Bible study video by teacher and writer Beth Moore, then have breakout groups. The first week, there were 100 adults, which surprised Rizor. She says, "God keeps telling me, 'You already have it.' This is his church, and he's going to build it. We just need to start from our strengths." Over 820 people ages two and older are in small groups at the church.

Rizor was sensitive to building on First Wesleyan's strengths, because she had seen what happened when others tried to squeeze the church into another mold. "They had tried to force the Willow Creek model on our church in a rigid way, with coaches and volunteer division leaders. The week I started, five of our seven division leaders quit. They were burned out. We had put the structure on volunteers who weren't ready and tried to build it from the top down. I believe a small groups ministry has to build from the bottom up," she emphasizes.

Today, Rizor avoids labels, even terms such as "small group," though that's what she is implementing in Sunday morning adult classes and throughout the church. She has started a monthly Leadership Community for worship and huddles and leads a discipleship group of potential leaders. "I'm not slapping labels like 'coach' or 'division leader' on them," she says. "I'm asking, 'Who's going to help me with this?' I really believe that people support that which they've helped to create."

As she and the senior pastor work to build First Wesleyan into a church of small groups, they try to take a long-term approach, both as they look to the future and appreciate the past. "What we're doing may seem new, and we're trying to move slowly but steadily," Rizor says. "A lot of people say this is a new thing for a Wesleyan church. But in the eighteenth century, Charles Wesley had small groups. If people go back and examine the roots of their church, they will find that the movement grew through small groups. This may seem new, but it is really a part of our heritage."

## The Start-Up Group Phase

Your leaders have modeled appropriate values during the model/turbo group phase. You've run new groups through a pilot phase to discover difficulties. Now you can give the "green light" to starting small groups throughout the church. The start-up group phase is the final phase before going public. You are now giving permission for interested people to develop groups and explore leadership.

During the start-up phase, you will need a training strategy so emerging groups and leaders can learn more skills. You will need regular leadership gatherings and an annual retreat. But this is still not the time to go public. It's too soon for weekly pulpit exhortations about joining small groups, because your structure isn't ready for the potential response.

Let's pick up where we left off in the story of Christian Assembly (C.A.) in Los Angeles. The church had finally settled on a meta model and gathered leaders for training. Their next step was to issue a broader invitation for people to try small groups once again. The senior pastor did a series on community and asked congregation members to fill out response cards if they wanted to be in a group. The response was again, overwhelming. "We realized, we're in trouble. How do we get leaders connected to people? No one—and I bought every book I could find on small groups—had given any direction on this," says Mark Guzman, small groups pastor.

Eventually, they decided to set up the groups geographically. "We got them into groups and thought we were done," Guzman says. "But about eighteen months into it, we hit a bump in the road. We didn't emphasize enough the role of coaches. We lost some coaches and leaders, and a key piece of that was simply a lack of coaching skills."

Guzman says one main difficulty was trying to squeeze C.A. into a model that might not fit. "We took a model, but we were not adjusting it to who we are," he said. "We believed small groups to be the catalyst for growth in our church." Despite the church's struggles, which are fairly normal, it now has 160 groups, enfolding about 1,200 adults and 400 children. Some of those groups don't have coaches and only 30 percent have apprentices, Guzman admits.

C.A., like most churches, is still in process. "We still need to bring health to our groups. We have some people who still don't believe in the value of groups, but then we also have lives that have been totally transformed. We are also redefining the coach's role," Guzman says. His next step is to do a turbo group with about twenty leaders. "We've also developed a health checklist for groups, based on our core values," he says. Adapting a model to a church's own values—that in itself is a giant step toward becoming a church of small groups.

Once you have run your first full ministry season, you'll want to stop and celebrate what happened during the start-up phase. This is the time to tell lots of stories and listen carefully to the experiences of your leaders and group members. You may want to do a survey or focus groups so that small group participants can share their experiences, both good and bad. Again, this is a time for learning and for refining your focus as a ministry.

## Going Public

In this final phase, your system is mature enough and you have enough leaders and groups to assimilate far more church members into small groups. We can't tell you exactly how many groups and leaders you need before going public, but don't ignore the issue. Many churches make the mistake of publicly announcing that everyone should participate in small groups—before enough systems, training, and leaders are in place. Most congregation members will wait a few months for you to find them a group. However, they won't wait much longer. If they respond to your public invitation but you can't connect them within three months, they will get frustrated. "Small groups don't work here," they will say.

If large numbers of people respond, you may need to create a "holding tank," usually a "taste of small groups" class that runs for several weeks. It gives people a place to connect while they're waiting to be assimilated into a small group. You need a holding tank so interest remains high and people can begin to experience true community.

Kevin Phillips, small groups director at Chicago's Park Community Church, understands this need for connection. About 100 of the 800 to 1,000 people who attend Park Community are young, single professionals in their early twenties. "Some of these people felt unconnected, and we didn't even realize it," Phillips said. "But now we have a group for them, called the Twenty-Somethings." The group was actually started by Chad

Peshak and Melissa Winslow, two Gen-Xers who wanted to connect with other people their own age in the church.

The group meets once a week. They spend some time together as a large group and then break into small groups. However, they still worship with the rest of the church at weekly services. "Small groups have defined what they are," Phillips said.

Unlike most of the other groups at Park, these groups have men and women together. "Throughout our church, we have always tended toward men and women having separate groups," Phillips said. "But these groups are mixed. I think the feeling of connection with people their own age is more important than a connection of gender."

The church also offers "Discovery Classes" so people can connect while learning about basic theology. "We have classes like 'New Testament Survey' or 'Principles of Stewardship,'" Phillips said. "It's a great way to get to meet people."

## Phasing in Groups in Small Traditional Churches

The phases we have described will look different in each setting. For Jeff Arnold, pastor of First Presbyterian Church in Beaver, Pennsylvania, the first step was just getting the people to think community. It's a difficult step in traditional churches, but Arnold found it can be done.

Arnold understood that geography matters more at his church than it might in other regions. Beaver is a small town outside Pittsburgh. "We're a mainline traditional small-town, East-coast church," Arnold says. "This area is declining in population. In the 1980s, western Pennsylvania lost 40 percent of its population. The steel mills shut down, and now, twenty years later, the area is just starting to recover economically. We are definitely not cutting edge. We are more like back edge."

During Arnold's first three-plus years as pastor, First Presbyterian has grown from 350 to 500 in worship attendance. Arnold says that's "wildly radical growth," considering the area's shrinking population and "militant townness." There are ten other Presbyterian churches, plus many from other denominations, within a four-mile radius of First Presbyterian. Yet people from each town have difficulty thinking of going to church in the next little town, even to one less than a mile away. Most nearby towns are surrounded by rivers and linked to other towns by bridges. Those bridges, Arnold says, are physical and psychological barriers that people simply don't cross.

Arnold recognized his congregation was entrenched. He understood its local culture. So he made change slowly. About 40 to 50 percent of the congregation participates in a combination of electives and small groups, "because I faked them out and didn't tell them," he jokes. He built on ministries such as Mothers of Preschoolers (MOPS) and Community Bible Study (CBS), an intensive study group that draws 370 people from various local congregations to weekly meetings.

"It's very content heavy, not as relational, but in the next few years, I think we're going to move more toward the meta style of groups," confides Arnold, who has written several books on small groups ministry, including *The Big Book on Small Groups* and *Small Group Outreach*. He gradually transitioned a hundred junior and senior high school students into a small-group-based youth ministry.

While moving slowly to build a church of small groups, Arnold has moved decisively to shake up his church's institutionalization. "I've been working to change the identity of the church," he says. "I'm trying to create a can-do atmosphere so people will have to think again. When I first got here, for example, the pastor was the only one who went to the hospital. Our congregation has fifty-five shut-ins. That's a lot. So when I go on visits, I take people with me. They are learning how to minister."

First Presbyterian's leaders had simply assigned people to committees, Arnold says, with little consideration of passion or giftedness. "My first meeting with the Christian Ed. board, I asked them what they liked about Christian education. They responded, 'We don't like it.' So I asked why they were doing it, and they said they had been told which committee to join," Arnold recalls. "So I looked at them and said with a grin, 'You're fired.' Then I started asking them what they wanted to do in the church, and they got nervous, saying things like, 'Where do you need me to serve?' I replied, 'Don't look for weakness or need. Look for call.' I'm a firm believer in the priesthood of all believers."

That philosophy has driven another area of growth for small groups. Serving teams are becoming small groups, and the church has made service a prerequisite for membership. "We don't let you join the church if you don't have a job to do here," he says.

Despite the unique challenges of western Pennsylvania culture, Arnold says he feels called to be right where he is. "My family loves living here," he says. "We love these people. When you enjoy people, they tend to enjoy you back."

Jeff Arnold's story should give you insight and hope. And he is not alone. It is happening everywhere that people believe community is worth the work, however long it takes.

## Signposts on the Road

Each phase on the way to going public takes prayer and preparation. Once you go public, the word is out and the real adventure begins. Again, no one can predict exactly what will take place. But in watching our own church embrace small groups and consulting with churches across North America, we have discovered some general principles.

You'll see definite trends as you move toward becoming a church of small groups. The priorities you'll face initially will be replaced by other issues as your groups mature. At first you'll need to focus on supervising leaders, providing centralized training, and planning large inspirational events. Gradually you'll ease up on supervision as lay leaders give input and assume responsibility. Highly controlled training will evolve into decentralized training as people learn from mentors and through shared experiences. People will begin to embrace and live out small group life, so they'll need fewer large events to sustain their energy for ministry.

While phasing in small groups, you'll shift focus. You'll see leadership confidence increase in each phase. You'll need more sophisticated tracking and evaluation systems to support more groups and leaders. Recruiting and developing leaders will take more time. When you first phase in small groups, you simply catalyze existing group leaders or those with leadership experience. But as your small group ministry matures, you'll need to find ways for veteran leaders to keep growing, and you'll need more new leaders.

One thing won't change. You will always have to manage the tension between leader readiness and community demand. It would be great to train every leader for eighteen months before they take over a small group. In most churches, however, the demand for community and need for shepherding require an accelerated leadership training process. Yes, this involves risk; yet, the greater risks may be alienating seekers or losing large groups of people. Leaders must discern how long they can train new leaders before launching them into the ministry. Again, remember Carl George's principle: the more supervision you provide, the less up-front training you need.

If you take the time to appropriately model leadership skills and character, then release leaders for pilot and start-up phases of experimentation and learning, you will be prepared to launch the ministry full scale. Remember, this is one ministry where speed kills. You definitely need to lead and be intentional and move people forward. However, you don't simply want to throw a bunch of groups together as quickly as possible. The results will be disastrous.

If you pay attention to each phase, you will be better prepared as you build a church of groups. We are confident that you can do it. Enjoy the journey.

# Closing Words

The pursuit of authentic Christian community through small groups is worth every ounce of energy you can give it. Community resides in the heart, nature, and character of God, is reflected in the life and ministry of Christ, is built into the relational DNA of every person, and, therefore, should be intentionally pursued as the structure for any local church. But it cannot be implemented as another program or system. Jesus gave his life to redeem a people, not restructure a program.

What takes place in each little community—each group—must produce people fully devoted to Christ and his redemptive mission. So groups must tenaciously pursue authentic relationships and courageously engage in discussions where the truth of God connects with each life to produce spiritual transformation. And when sin gets the best of us and cracks begin to form in the relational foundation of a group, healthy conflict resolution becomes the mandatory curriculum used to foster biblical reconciliation.

Because these communities can be fragile and complex, leaders are needed to guide them along the pathway to life in the kingdom. These leaders intentionally shepherd their flocks like King David, with integrity of heart and with skillful hands (Psalm 78:72). Leaders recognize that they are the vital link between church members and church staff. They understand the responsibility and thrill of participating in the community-building ministry of Christ.

But if we are to do justice in helping these shepherds fulfill the calling and ministry given them by God, we must train and support them with the best resources at our disposal. Coaching becomes a necessity, not a luxury, and leadership development becomes the responsibility of everyone, not just a select few. If groups are to flourish, they must be well led and members must be well tended.

Finally, church leaders must face the challenges of moving from a church with groups to a church *of* groups. Strategic leadership decisions must be made and lots of questions have to be answered. Your church must ruthlessly evaluate its ministry in light of the resources available and the culture to which you are called. Phasing in the small group transition will take time, prayer, and lots of grace. You will undoubtedly make several trips back to the drawing board. But for the sake of the people under your care—and those you've yet to enfold—please don't give up. Be tenacious and stay in the game.

If you want to live in the Chicagoland area, you have to get used to the roads. As we often say here, "We have only two seasons—winter and construction." If you're a baseball fan and want to experience the thrill of a White Sox victory, you have to drive on the Kennedy or Eisenhower Expressways to get to a game, and in summer that means highway repairs and an occasional disabled vehicle or accident to create a traffic nightmare. It can be a long ride—more than you'd planned. But it's all worth it when you walk into the stadium with your twelve-year-old son and his eyes light up like a Christmas tree when he sees the ball field, smells the popcorn, grabs a hot dog and watches his favorite players battle it out on the ball diamond. You look at each other and smile. The Kennedy Expressway is a distant memory.

If you want to navigate the roads of building a church of small groups, you had better get some new tires and a fresh set of shock absorbers. It's a bumpy ride with lots of turns, a few potholes, and an occasional accident, and the expressway is always under construction. But the prize at the end of the highway is well worth fighting some traffic jams along the way. Today we just simply cannot imagine our church without group life, without the countless stories of transformation and growth because people gathered in the name of Christ to live out the many "one another" commands in the Bible. The road has been difficult, but the reward is well worth it. So are you willing to make the trip? Willing to do the work and stay the course?

Speaking to a group of church leaders about small groups, Bill Hybels made the following comments. They provide a fitting end to this book (but not to our story, because it goes on for eternity). Bill's words describe why we feel so committed to this cause. And we hope that if our words failed along the way, perhaps his will cause you to consider the kingdom opportunity that lies just around the bend for your church.

If the sight of a once solo-minded man or woman who never shared a feeling or disclosed a secret to anybody in his or her life is now sitting in a circle of caring brothers and sisters freely giving and receiving love—if the sight of that person sitting around that circle stirs something deep within you, then you ought to give what's left of the rest of your life to the small groups revolution that God is orchestrating in his church worldwide.

If the thought of moving a freshly redeemed but clueless brand new Christian into an established group of mature believers who are going to love that person and nurture him and push his roots down deep into the soil of faith—if that thought floods you with energy and passion, then you ought to rearrange your life and join the rest of us who are waving the flag of Christian community and inviting people into small circles of fellowship.

If the picture of six people standing around a hospital bed holding hands and singing worship songs as their apprentice leader loses her two-year fight against cancer and dies before their eyes—if the picture around that hospital bed grips your heart and quickens your pulse, then cancel your plans.

Find a way to join those of us on the front lines of the small groups battle and get yourself into the fray. And if at the end of your life it is enough for you to stand before the glorified Christ and hear him say, "Well done son, well done daughter, you gave your life for the very cause I gave mine—community—well done"; if the thought of that ignites your spirit and sets your soul a soaring, then you're a goner. Just give it up! You might as well get it over with right now!

Join the ragtag under-resourced idealistic band of relational rebels who still believe—perhaps rather naively—that two are better than one, that a cord of three strands will never be broken, that what we can do together in the church of Jesus Christ is a hundred times what any of us can do alone. If that's you, give the best that you could give, give the best days of what's left of the rest of your life for this small groups revolution and the very cause that Jesus imagined in John 17— that his followers would be *one*. Will you do it? Will you give yourself to that?

We hope you will—that you will give the best that you can to building a church where nobody stands alone. Not now. Not ever.

# Appendix 1

# Willow Creek Small Group
# Facts at a Glance

Note: Our structure is patterned after the "Meta-Church" model as described in the book *Prepare Your Church for the Future* by Carl George (Grand Rapids: Baker, 1991).

| | |
|---|---|
| **Size of Groups** | Approximately 4–10 people with an average of about 8 (groups that get bigger than ten eventually birth into two or more daughter groups) |
| **Leadership of Groups** | Trained lay leader and an apprentice leader (apprentice leaders are preparing to lead their own group someday) |
| **Frequency of Meetings** | Some monthly; most 2–3 times per month; many others (especially task groups) meet weekly |
| **Curriculum** | Leaders and members decide (some popular examples: The Serendipity Bible, the New Community series, Bible 101, the Walking with God series, the Interactions Series, and Tough Questions) |
| **Location** | Varies, although most meet in homes; some rotate, some remain in one home; members decide who will host the meeting(s) |
| **Duration** | Depends on purpose; many recovery groups last 9 weeks; kids groups last for the school year; adult groups last 3–5 years, depending on whether they birth a new group |
| **Attendees** | Most groups are "open" (that is, they have a core membership but encourage the use of the "open chair" to allow for newcomers) |
| **Types of Small Groups** | • Age/stage-based (couples, singles, men's, women's, children, youth)<br>• Task-based (groups that meet around the fulfillment of a task or volunteer ministry)<br>• Interest-based (seeker groups designed for nonbelievers to investigate the faith, other interests)<br>• Care-based (such as AA, ACOA, grief recovery, divorce recovery) |
| **Oversight of Groups** | All group leaders have a lay "coach," who oversees up to five groups; coaches are led by a staff "division leader," who shepherds up to ten coaches |
| **Statistics** | 2,700 groups, approximately 18,000 people in groups; approximately 3,500 leaders and coaches |

(as of 5/31/01)

## Appendix 2

# Kinds of Small Groups
# at Willow Creek

In becoming a church of groups we have provided our people with a broad range of group options. This allows people to enter into group life at a place that is appropriate for their spiritual growth and development. We can provide this freedom and flexibility because of two major commitments: a commitment to the 5 G's (a common framework) and to a common structure (the adapted meta model, where each leader is shepherded by a coach). In this way, regardless of the primary focus or mission of a particular group, each group can be challenged to pursue growth in a way consistent with our church philosophy and strategy for making disciples.

## Affinity

Groups at Willow Creek are organized around "affinities"—that is, those things that they have in common. This is not an attempt to make groups exclusive or narrow, but rather a means of initially organizing groups so that it is relatively easy for anyone in any stage of life or maturity to find a small group. In reality, even when we think we have much in common with others, we soon discover that we are very different in many ways. At that point, the challenge to become a Christian community must be met with love and resolve and intention.

There are four major small group affinities under which almost any kind of group might fall: age/stage-based, interest-based, task-based, or care-based. Here are some examples of each.

### Age/Stage-Based Groups

Most churches utilize this organizing framework in some way, whether it is in Sunday school classes or small groups. At Willow Creek these include groups for singles, couples, men, women, children, and youth. In addition, our Axis ministry to twenty-somethings has a robust small group structure. Within some of these areas there are other affinities (marketplace men, moms groups, young married couples, etc.). Some groups may have a broad age range (a men's or a women's group) while others may form around a more common life stage (single moms). Many of the adult groups meet off campus in homes, restaurants, offices, or community centers. Some meet at the church, especially around a teaching event (such as women participating in some of our women's Bible classes during the week).

Children in our Promiseland ministry (our Sunday school) are in small groups from age three through fifth grade. Classes have "large group" time, where there is a Bible lesson and some activities; then they break into small groups, each with an adult leader. It is exciting for us to see our kids growing up in groups with an adult committed to shepherding our kids alongside of us. Junior high (Sonlight) and senior high (Student Impact) small groups are organized by school district so that kids can connect during the week away from church as friends. Most of these groups meet during the youth gatherings, though as kids get older more meetings take place off campus.

## Interest-Based Groups

These groups are organized by areas of common interest, such as Bible study or prayer. In other cases the affinity is a common skill or focus of employment, such as our computer connection (which has spawned several small groups) or medical professionals. In each case a leader may have a passion for reaching a certain group of people and enfolding them into community. A common interest—work, a hobby, a field of knowledge—is merely the organizing principle. In this case, there can be quite a variety of ages and both genders represented, since the affinity will appeal to all people (like an interest in computers). Each group is still required to have a trained leader guiding people toward spiritual maturity and providing a place for them in community with others in the church.

One unique interest-based group is the Seeker Small Group. These groups provide a safe but engaging place for people who have questions about Christianity or who are open to spiritual discussions. Led by a believer, these groups help guide seekers to the truth of Scripture while also providing a forum for discussion and even disagreement. People can pursue answers to their spiritual questions or problems while observing the transformation that takes place in others as they come to faith in Christ. These groups usually last from six months to a year.

## Task-Based Groups

When members share a common desire to serve others, it presents an opportunity to build community and meet the needs of people. Such serving groups are organized around special needs, such as helping the poor or working with our inner-city extension ministry teams. In other cases, it is something related to work around our church, such as ushering, parking teams, food preparation and service, building and grounds care, or something unique like our cars ministry. The Willow Creek Cars Ministry provided cars for over two hundred single parents last year, and provides lifetime free care for those vehicles. It is run by eleven small groups of volunteer mechanics. Over a thousand used vehicles were donated by Willow Creek church members, many of which are sold to buy parts to repair other vehicles. Doing a task together promotes a servant spirit and allows people to build Christlike community while working alongside one another.

## Care-Based Groups

Finally, there are groups whose primary purpose is to provide care and support for people who are in the midst of a crisis or need help overcoming sinful patterns of behavior, namely, addictions. Such groups include grief recovery (loss of a loved one) and divorce recovery (Rebuilders). In addition there is Pathfinders (for chronic illnesses), the Prayer Ministry, the Willow Creek Food Pantry, Special Friends (for developmentally challenged persons), Heritage (assisting those in nursing homes), Christians in Recovery (for those overcoming alcohol and chemical dependency), and A Safe Place (for those struggling with same sex attractions). These groups provide a caring community and a place for many at our church to serve.

## Frequently Asked Questions

*How do serving groups also build community?* It is a challenge, but one that we are committed to. Some groups meet briefly before or after the task for connection and prayer, and get more of the Bible teaching from other classes at Willow or our main services. Others do their tasks one week and meet as a small group the next. Still others are able to meet for thirty to forty-five minutes in and around their task, using both the group time and the task time as tools to build community.

*What do your children's groups do?* In large group time the Bible lesson is taught creatively with activities and drama. When kids go to their small groups (anywhere from twenty to forty minutes) they look at the passage more closely, memorize Bible verses, pray for each other, and build relationships under the care of an adult leader.

*Do all your groups do Bible study?* Formal Bible study is done mostly in the age/stage-based groups and interest-based groups. Couples groups, men's groups, women's groups, and singles groups tend to spend more time together in meetings and can devote more time to Bible study. Interest-based groups spend some time in Bible study but also tend to serve together from time to time. Task-based groups do some study, but it varies depending on the demand of the task and the time allotted for it. Care-based groups tend to gather first in larger groups for teaching, then break into small groups for discussion, sharing, and prayer.

*Do all your groups ever do the same curriculum?* Because of the variety of groups and purposes, it would be difficult and perhaps even counterproductive to do the same curriculum. However, we do have seasons of emphasis when our entire church is focused on a common theme, like evangelism or spiritual disciplines. In such cases we make a broad recommendation to the congregation and provide materials for groups to use. Many take advantage of this—though not usually the highly focused recovery groups and some task groups. We also develop a small group discussion tool from our teaching each week at New Community, our mid-week service where we participate in the sacraments, teach the Bible, and have extended singing and worship.

# Notes

### Introduction: The Willow Creek Story
1. Dietrich Bonhoeffer, *Life Together* (New York: Harper & Row, 1954), p. 21.

### Chapter 1. In the Beginning, God: The Theological Evidence
1. Gareth Icenogle, *Biblical Foundations for Small Group Ministry* (Downers Grove, Ill.: InterVarsity, 1994), p. 13.

2. John McCain, *Faith of My Fathers* (New York: Random House, 1999), p. 209.

3. Dallas Willard, *The Divine Conspiracy* (San Francisco: Harper San Francisco, 1998), p. 318.

4. Peterson delivered this sermon in the United States. If he had been preaching in another country, he would, presumably, have substituted "all Brazilians" or "all Chinese" to reflect his audience's context.

5. Their words, not mine.

6. Gilbert Bilezikian, *Community 101* (Grand Rapids: Zondervan, 1997), p. 37.

### Chapter 3. What the Church Needs to Grow: The Organizational Evidence
1. Carl George, *Nine Keys to Effective Small Group Leadership* (Mansfield, Pa.: Kingdom, 1997), p. 196.

2. Many scholars follow the counting of Numbers, which lists more than 600,000 fighting men, and therefore derive a minimum estimate of the total number of the Israelites to be at least two million.

### Chapter 4. Small Groups Are Built on Authentic Relationships

1. Larry Crabb, *The Safest Place on Earth* (Dallas: Word, 1999), p. xiii.

2. Henri Nouwen, *In the Name of Jesus* (New York: Crossroad/ Herder & Herder, 1993), p. 43.

3. Julie Gorman, *Community That Is Christian* (Colorado Springs: Chariot Victor, 1993), p. 98.

4. Michael Christiansen, ed., *Equipping the Saints* (Nashville: Abingdon, 2000), p. 50.

5. Parker Palmer, *To Know As We Are Known* (San Francisco: Harper San Francisco, 1993), p. 8.

6. Nouwen, *The Living Reminder* (San Francisco: Harper and Row, n.d.), p. 13.

7. Henry Cloud, *Changes That Heal* (Grand Rapids: Zondervan, 1993), pp. 79–80.

8. Icenogle, *Biblical Foundations*, p. 69.

### Chapter 5. Small Groups Are Places Where Truth Meets Life

1. Willow Creek family groups may include singles, childless couples, or entire families. They often meet for three or four hours, including a meal, once or twice a month, as well as in between official meetings.

2. We produce a monthly tape series entitled "Defining Moments," distributed to churches that are members of the Willow Creek Association. These "moments" are pivotal in the life of a church, group, or leader and result in profound change and awareness of God's power and presence.

3. Nouwen, *Making All Things New* (San Francisco: Harper San Francisco, 1998), p. 82.

4. Margaret Guenther, *The Practice of Prayer* (Boston: Cowley, 1998), p. 39.

### Chapter 6. Small Groups Experience Healthy Conflict

1. David Augsburger, *Caring Enough to Confront* (Ventura, Calif.: Gospel Light, 1981), p. 12.

2. For more on covenants, see pp. 85–89 in *Leading Life-Changing Small Groups* by Bill Donahue (Grand Rapids: Zondervan, 1996).

3. John Ortberg, *The Life You've Always Wanted* (Grand Rapids: Zondervan, 1997), p. 122.

4. Gordon MacDonald, *Mid-Course Correction* (Nashville: Thomas Nelson, 2000), 37.

5. For further insights into the process of forgiveness we recommend the teaching of Lewis B. Smedes, *Forgive and Forget: Healing the Hurts We Don't Deserve* (San Francisco: Harper San Francisco, 1996 [reprint]) and *The Art of Forgiving* (New York: Ballantine Books, 1997).

## Chapter 7. Small Groups Provide Well-Balanced Shepherding

1. Nouwen, *In the Name of Jesus*, pp. 42–43.

2. Palmer, *The Active Life: A Spirituality of Work, Creativity, and Caring* (San Francisco: Jossey-Bass, 1999), p. 31.

3. Nouwen, *In the Name of Jesus*, pp. 40–41.

4. Bilezikian, *Community 101*, p. 66.

5. Nouwen, *Life of the Beloved* (New York: Crossroad/Herder & Herder, 1992), p. 90.

## Chapter 8. Enlisting Small Group Leaders

1. Guenther, *The Practice of Prayer*, p. 7.

## Chapter 11. Make Decisions

1. See, for example, Alan Nelson, Gene Appel, Jim Mellado, and Bill Hybels, *How to Change Your Church without Killing It* (Nelson: Word, 2001); Everett Rodgers, *Diffusion of Innovation* (New York: The Free Press, 1962), and John P. Kotter, *Leading Change* (Cambridge, Mass.: Harvard Business School, 1996).

## Chapter 12. Choose a Strategy

1. Greg Ogden, *The New Reformation* (Grand Rapids: Zondervan, 1992), pp. 11–12.

# WILLOW
### Willow Creek Association

# Willow Creek Association
*Vision, Training, Resources for Prevailing Churches*

This resource was created to serve you and to help you build a local church that prevails. It is just one of many ministry tools that are part of the Willow Creek Resources® line, published by the Willow Creek Association together with Zondervan.

The Willow Creek Association (WCA) was created in 1992 to serve a rapidly growing number of churches from across the denominational spectrum that are committed to helping unchurched people become fully devoted followers of Christ. Membership in the WCA now numbers over 10,500 Member Churches worldwide from more than ninety denominations.

The Willow Creek Association links like-minded Christian leaders with each other and with strategic vision, training, and resources in order to help them build prevailing churches designed to reach their redemptive potential. Here are some of the ways the WCA does that.

- **A2: Building Prevailing Acts 2 Churches—Today**—an annual two-and-a-half day event, held at Willow Creek Community Church in South Barrington, Illinois, to explore strategies for building churches that reach out to seekers and build believers, and to discover new innovations and breakthroughs from Acts 2 churches around the country.

- **The Leadership Summit**—a once a year, two-and-a-half-day conference to envision and equip Christians with leadership gifts and responsibilities. Presented live at Willow Creek as well as via satellite broadcast to over one hundred locations across North America, this event is designed to increase the leadership effectiveness of pastors, ministry staff, volunteer church leaders, and Christians in the marketplace.

- **Ministry-Specific Conferences**—throughout each year the WCA hosts a variety of conferences and training events—both at Willow Creek's main campus and offsite, across the U.S., and around the world—targeting church leaders and volunteers in ministry-specific areas such as: evangelism, small groups, preaching and teaching, the arts, children, students, women, volunteers, stewardship, raising up resources, etc.

- **Willow Creek Resources®**—provides churches with trusted and field-tested ministry resources in such areas as leadership, evangelism, spiritual formation, spiritual gifts, small groups, stewardship, student ministry, children's ministry, the use of the arts-drama, media, contemporary music —and more.

- **WCA Member Benefits**—includes substantial discounts to WCA training events, a 20 percent discount on all Willow Creek Resources®, *Defining Moments* monthly audio journal for leaders, quarterly *Willow* magazine, access to a Members-Only section on WillowNet, monthly communications, and more. Member Churches also receive special discounts and premier services through WCA's growing number of ministry partners—Select Service Providers—and save an average of $500 annually depending on the level of engagement.

For specific information about WCA conferences, resources, membership, and other ministry services contact:

**Willow Creek Association**
P.O. Box 3188
Barrington, IL 60011-3188
Phone: 847-570-9812
Fax: 847-765-5046
www.willowcreek.com

We want to hear from you. Please send your comments about this book to us in care of zreview@zondervan.com. Thank you.

Deposit Check
Write Out Testimony
Call About Jenis Party
Watch Tutorial Vid

Read Book